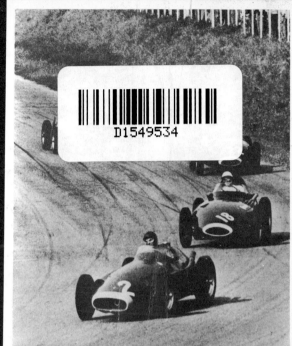

HISTORIC MOTOR RACING

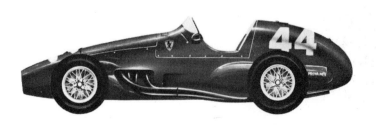

ANTHONY PRITCHARD

HISTORIC MOTOR RACING

WEIDENFELD AND NICOLSON
5 WINSLEY STREET LONDON W1

Acknowledgements

The author would like to express his gratitude to Keith Davey for his assistance in the preparation of this book.

The author and publishers are greatly indebted to the following owners and agencies by whose kind permission the illustrations are reproduced: Autocar, 44, 46, 49, 70; Auto Union ZMBH, 31, 47; Lt. Col. C. H. D. Berthon, 14; H. G. Conway, 11, 15, 17; Daimler-Benz AG, 13, 32, 40, 41, 42, 43, 48; Keith Duerden, 118; L'Editrice dell'Automobile, 62; J. Herbert Elliott, 54, 55; Edward Eves, 130, 131; Fiat (England) Ltd., 4; Geoffrey Goddard, 114, 115; Guy Griffiths, 8, 10, 18, 19, 21, 22, 23, 26, 27, 33, 34, 38, 56, 58, 59, 64, 65, 67, 68, 73, 74, 75, 76, 77, 78, 81, 82, 83, 84, 85, 86, 87, 88, 90, 91, 92, 93, 97, 98, 99, 103, 104, 108, 110; Indianapolis Motor Speedway Museum, 51, 52, 57, 60, 61; Louis Klementaski, 37, 39, 45, 53, 79, 80, 94, 120; Leica Studio Wörner, 117; T. C. March, 100, 101, 102, 113, 119, 122, 123, 124, 126, 127, 132, 133; Jeremy Mason, 5; Montagu Motor Museum, 6, 9; Motor, 28; Motor Sport, 50, 112, 121, 125, 128, 129; Officine Alfieri Maserati, 36; Cyril Posthumus, 12; Profile Publications Ltd., 1; Publifoto, Milan, 2, 66, 72, 95; Radio Times Hulton Picture Library, 3, 24; Times, 35; Vantage Photography, 20, 25, 29, 30, 69, 71, 96, 105, 106, 107, 109, 111, 116; from the author's collection, 7, 16, 63, 89.

(*page* 1) The 1955 Tipo 625 Ferrari.
(*frontispiece*) The line-up for the 1936 Italian Grand Prix. Nos. 6 and 8 are the works Auto Unions, while behind them are three 8C-35 Alfa Romeos of the Scuderia Ferrari.

SBN 297 76376 8
© 1969 by Anthony Pritchard
Designed by Behram Kapadia for George Weidenfeld and Nicolson Limited
Printed by Fleming & Humphreys (Baylis) Ltd., Leicester

Contents

5

CHAPTER ONE

Introduction

THE first officially recognised competition between motor vehicles was the Paris-Rouen run of 1894, won by the Comte de Dion's steam tractor. A year later, Emile Levassor with his Panhard et Levassor won the first genuine motor *race*, held over a distance of 732 miles from Paris to Bordeaux and back. Full-scale long-distance races achieved wide popularity on the continent, and in 1901 the new 'Mercedes' changed the concept of the 'horseless carriage' to the motor-car. William Maybach, who designed the car for the German Daimler concern, scrapped the notion of a wooden chassis frame in favour of a pressed steel chassis, introduced the 'gate-change' gearbox still used today, produced an engine that was quieter and more flexible than any of its rivals and improved both stability and appearance by the use of evenly sized wheels front and rear.

Thus the Mercedes set a trend which its rivals were forced to follow – sooner or, in some cases, later. During the next two years trans-continental racing was keenly supported by motor manufacturers, established or merely aspiring to fame, and spectator enthusiasm reached a fever pitch which culminated in the disastrous and horrifying Paris-Madrid event of 1903. At Bordeaux the race was brought to an unplanned halt, leaving in its wake a trail of shattered cars and a carnage of dead drivers and spectators, the result of totally inadequate crowd control. Racing continued on closed circuits, usually public roads, with the spectators well away from the track, with such events as the Grand Prix in France, the forebear of all later Grands Prix and held between 1906 and 1908 and from 1912 onwards, and

3 (*opposite*) From an earlier age – a 1912 7·6-litre Peugeot driven by Malcolm Campbell at Brooklands in 1923.

the German Kaiserpreis of 1907. These races continued to attract many and varied entries and technical innovations from the more inspired. Early Grand Prix regulations encouraged cars of vast engine capacity such as the 16-litre Fiat of 1905, and as late as 1912 Fiats were racing 15-litre cars. There were, however, constructors who were thinking in terms of low-weight and high-efficiency engines and significant among these was the Isotta Fraschini voiturette of 1908, a design in which it is believed the young Ettore Bugatti had a hand and then incorporated many of its features in his 1,327 cc (65 × 100 mm) 4-cylinder single overhead camshaft car which took second place in the 1911 Grand Prix de France (a race not to be confused with the Grand Prix itself).

In 1914 the Mercedes entered for the Grand Prix at Lyons represented the latest in racing car design, although it did not possess the front wheel brakes or twin overhead camshafts of the rival Peugeots. The general design was slim and compact, and the 4-cylinder engine, influenced by the design of the Company's aero engines, had four valves per cylinder inclined at an angle of sixty degrees, a single overhead camshaft and, to ensure complete combustion, three sparking plugs per cylinder. Power output was a claimed 115 bhp at 2,800 rpm. In the race the Mercedes took the first three places, defeating opposition from Peugeot, Delage, Fiat and Sunbeam.

The outbreak of war four weeks later brought racing to a halt and there was no resumption until 1919. The war had, however, taught many lessons in metallurgy, design and production, gained primarily from the manufacture of aero engines. One of the most successful of these had been Bugatti's aero engine produced both as a straight-eight and as a 16-cylinder by mounting the blocks on a common crankcase. It was this 8-cylinder arrangement that was adopted on the immediate post-war 5-litre Duesenbergs and Ballots which met at Indianapolis in 1921 and the same classic arrangement powered the Mercedes-Benz W 196 of 1954-5. For 1920 a 3-litre engine capacity limit was adopted at Indianapolis, and in Europe a year later.

The first post-war Grand Prix was held at Le Mans in 1921

4 The 8-cylinder 3-litre Tipo 802 Fiat of the type which took third place in the 1921 Italian Grand Prix. It is seen here with Bordino at the wheel.

and was won convincingly by Jimmy Murphy's Duesenberg, a car of which more will be heard later in this book. Among the Duesenberg's technical innovations was the use for the first time in a Grand Prix of hydraulic brakes, but with a mixture of glycerin and water instead of the familiar brake fluid of today. A year later a 2,000 cc Formula was adopted and the straight-eight Ballot, Fiat and Sunbeams were rendered obsolescent after a year's racing. The Ballots were the work of Ernest Henry, who had pioneered the twin overhead camshaft cylinder head and had appeared at Indianapolis in 1920; it was on the design of these that the 1921 Sunbeam was based and these British cars were subsequently raced, in improved form, in the 1922 Tourist Trophy.

In 1922 five contenders appeared in Grand Prix racing: Ballot, Bugatti, Rolland-Pilain, Fiat, the great trend-setter of the twenties, and Sunbeam, the great imitator. While the French Rolland-Pilain concern and Bugatti, who clothed his cars in individualistic streamlined bodies, still favoured the 8-cylinder layout, Fiat as a matter of convenience redesigned the 3-litre car as a 2-litre 6-cylinder, and Sunbeam persuaded Henry to design for them a disastrously unsuccessful 4-cylinder model. The Fiats were devastatingly superior and during the next few

5 (*above*) The well-instrumented dash of the 3-litre Sunbeam. Note the large-diameter steering wheel and the ignition retard and advance in the centre of the wheel.

6 (*below*) The 3-litre 8-cylinder Sunbeam, a Fiat-inspired design, with which Jean Chassagne won the 1922 Tourist Trophy held in the Isle of Man.

years led the design field in Grand Prix racing. For 1923 the Turin concern reverted to an 8-cylinder layout and pioneered the racing of supercharged cars. They retired from Grand Prix racing at the end of 1924 but returned, briefly and successfully, in 1927, with a 1½-litre 12-cylinder car which had its cylinders in two vertical banks and two side-by-side crankshafts. This had a power output of 175 bhp at 7,500 rpm and won the 1927 Milan Grand Prix with complete ease, but was never raced again.

Diversity was the mark of both the STD and the Delage concerns. As well as racing 1½-litre voiturettes under the Darracq and Talbot banners during the twenties, the STD group raced in 1923 Sunbeams directly copied from the previous year's Fiats and the work of Bertarione, a former Fiat employee. For 1924, again imitating Fiat practice, the cars were supercharged. In 1923 Segrave, driving a Sunbeam, won the French Grand Prix at Tours and the following year scored a victory at San Sebastian, Britain's last Grand Prix victory for over thirty years. A 2-litre Sunbeam still appears in Vintage Sports Car Club events, as does the V-12 4-litre supercharged Sunbeam 'Tiger' of 1926 [figure 27] which was raced by Segrave in both races and sprints and rebuilt for Malcolm Campbell in 1931.

The Delage contributions to racing commenced with two 5-litre 6-cylinder cars for use in sprints and hill-climbs and a

7 (above) One of three very unusual cars entered by Bugatti in the 1922 French Grand Prix at Strasbourg. They were based on the 8-cylinder 2-litre Type 30 touring model, but were fitted with this bulbous streamlined bodywork.

8 (left) Another record-breaking car still being used is the 10½-litre Delage which in 1923 covered the flying mile at Arpajon at 143·24 mph.

year later there followed a massive 10½-litre 280 bhp car [figure 8], the career of which included sprints and hill-climbs, a successful attempt on the world's land speed record and in 1932 a victory by John Cobb in the British Empire Trophy at Brooklands. Delage entered Grand Prix racing in 1923 with a tremendously complicated V-12 design which in 1925 super-charged form won both the French and the Spanish Grands Prix. When a 1½-litre Formula was introduced for 1926, Louis Delage raced a straight-eight design of 1,495 cc which dominated the Grand Prix scene in 1926 and 1927. It was one of these cars in rebuilt form that Dick Seaman used so effectively to defeat the latest ERAs and Maseratis nine years later. One of the most remarkable features of Delage history is that so many of these racing cars have survived and can still be seen racing in Vintage Sports Car Club events.

One of the most important designs of the twenties was the P2 Alfa Romeo, which was the work of Vittorio Jano, another former Fiat engineer who had left the Company to design a car incorporating a large number of Fiat features. This twin overhead camshaft, straight-eight 1,987 cc design first appeared in 1924, winning that year's Italian Grand Prix, and in 1925 scored victories at Spa, Montlhéry and Monza. Although Alfa Romeo did not enter the cars after 1925, they continued to be

9 The 8-cylinder P2 Alfa Romeo Grand Prix car was designed by Vittorio Jano; the model achieved a great deal of success in 1924-5. Count Brilli-Peri is at the wheel.

raced until 1930 and features of the design appeared in both later production and racing Alfas. 1926 saw the appearance of the first Maserati, a straight-eight twin overhead camshaft car of 1½-litres, and it was these two makes, together with the Bugatti Type 35, that were to be the mainstay of racing for the next few years.

The Type 35 Bugatti had first appeared in 1924 and, apart from its designer's unwillingness to use twin overhead camshafts, represented all that was best in the racing car of the twenties. It set the trend that was to be followed until the introduction of the 750 kilogramme Formula in 1934 and it was one of the most beautiful racing cars of all time. The engine was a superbly constructed and proportioned supercharged straight-eight of 1,990 cc (60 × 88 mm), 1,493 cc (52 × 88 mm) or 2,261 cc (60 × 100 mm). The latter two variants were known as

10 The 8-cylinder single overhead camshaft engine of the 2·3-litre Type 35B Bugatti.

the Types 39 and 35B. In addition Bugatti marketed the 35A which had plain instead of roller bearings for the crankshaft and the Type 37 which had a plain bearing 4-cylinder engine of 1,496 cc derived directly from that powering the car which had finished second in the 1911 Grand Prix de France. The Type 35, however, was probably the most outstanding racing car of the twenties and its successes were innumerable.

11 The 1½-litre Type 39 supercharged Bugatti of Joules Goux making a pit stop in/the 1926 Spanish Grand Prix at San Sebastian. He won the race at an average speed of 70·53 mph.

CHAPTER TWO

Racing Without Restrictions 1928-33

AFTER the exciting racing of the previous years, Grand Prix racing took a disappointing turn in 1928 with the introduction of an ineffective Formula which simply imposed a minimum weight of 550 kg and a maximum of 750 kg. The net result was that the vast majority of races were run on a *Formule Libre* basis. The racing scene was made even duller by the withdrawal from racing of such concerns as the Sunbeam-Talbot-Darracq organisation, Fiat and Delage. Racing was mainly dominated during the years 1928-30 by the Bugatti Type 35, with interventions from Maserati, Alfa Romeo and some of the faster sports cars. The Bugattis and Maseratis were unchanged from the cars which raced in 1927 and the Alfa Romeos were P2 models which had raced so successfully during the 1924 and 1925 seasons and had subsequently been used in *Formule Libre* events. P2s scored a total of seven wins in the years 1928-9, and for 1930 four cars were in fact rebuilt by the Alfa works. The cars were now distinguished by sloping radiators similar to those of the current production 1750 Grand Sport model, parts from which were incorporated in the chassis, and the engines were enlarged to 2,006 cc (61·5 × 85 mm) giving a power output of 175 bhp. Survivors of the model in 1924 form can be seen at the Alfa Romeo Museum in Arese near Milan and in 1930 form in the Biscaretti Museum in Turin.

For the years 1929-30 the Grand Prix Formula was revised and the following restrictions were imposed: (1) Not more than 14 kg of fuel and oil to be used per 100 kilometres (equivalent to 14½ mpg); (2) a minimum weight of not less than 900 kg; (3)

12 (*opposite*) Line-up of the entries for the 1933 Penya Rhin Grand Prix held in Montjuich Park, Barcelona. From left to right of the picture are Nacional Pescara of Esteban Tort, the Type 51 Bugatti of Marcel Lehoux and the Monza Alfa Romeos of Wimille and Nuvolari.

13 Caracciola's winning Mercedes in the 1931 Avusrennen – a fine performance by a stripped sports car in a racing car event.

two-seater bodies of not less than 100 cm in width to be fitted. In 1929 commercial fuel had to be used, but up to 30 per cent benzole was allowed the following year. These regulations were also largely ineffective and racing continued to be held on a *Formule Libre* basis without any notable technical developments.

One result of this was the intrusion into the Grand Prix scene of what were basically sports cars. The Mercedes Company fielded their enormous 7,069 cc (100 × 150 mm) 6-cylinder single overhead camshaft 38/250 SSKL (*Super Sports Kurz Leicht*) models in both racing and sports events, and these now legendary cars achieved notable successes in both fields. Caracciola was third in the 1929 Monaco Grand Prix, a race over a difficult circuit for which the SSKL could hardly be less suited, and in 1931 won both the German Grand Prix and the Avusrennen [figure 13]. For 1932, Mercedes produced a pure racing version with a highly streamlined body. Special track versions of the Bentley, primarily for use at Brooklands, achieved a fair degree of success in their own sphere and one, Tim Birkin's 4½-litre supercharged single-seater, still makes regular appearances in Vintage Sports Car Club events. Britain's greatest racing car, as opposed to sports car success, however, was in the 1930 French Grand Prix at Pau. The entry consisted largely of Bugattis, but Birkin, driving a supercharged 4½-litre

sports Bentley [figure 14] stripped of all unnecessary equipment, succeeded in taking second place a mere three minutes behind the winning Bugatti.

One new car did, however, make an appearance during the 1929 season. This was the *Sedici Cilindri* Maserati, which was a fearsome device consisting of two of the existing 2-litre Maserati engines mated and mounted alongside each other, with the exhaust ports on the outside, in a strengthened and lengthened chassis. On its first appearance, at the Circuit of Cremona, held on a very fast circuit, it was driven by Baconin Borzacchini, and over a 10-kilometre straight it was timed at 152·9 mph, a new International record. It did, however, retire in both this event and the Monza Grand Prix, where in its heat it finished second to Momberger's Mercedes-Benz SSK. At this time the initiative in Grand Prix racing was being taken by Maserati and a further new model was introduced by the Bologna concern for 1930. This was a completely revised version of the 8-cylinder design, with a capacity of 2,495 cc (65 × 94 mm), and, on a 7·5 : 1 compression ratio, a power output of 175 bhp was developed at 6,000 rpm. The new car proved vastly superior to the Type 35 Bugatti and P2 Alfa Romeo opposition and during the 1930 season Maseratis won a total of seven major races which included a victory by Borzacchini in the Tripoli Grand Prix with

14 The running of Grand Prix racing to *Formule Libre* rules resulted in the appearance of some rather odd machinery. This is Birkin's stripped Le Mans sports 4½-litre Bentley in the 1930 French Grand Prix at Pau. Birkin took second place to a pure racing Bugatti at an average of 88·50 mph.

15 (*above*) The 16-cylinder Bugatti used in hill climbs and sprints during 1930. Chiron is seen driving the car in the Klausen Hill Climb.
16 (*right*) This privately owned Type 51 Bugatti was driven in the 1931 French Grand Prix at Montlhéry by Lehoux and Etancelin. They retired in this ten-hour race after having covered 188 miles.

the *Sedici Cilindri*. The 8C-2500 scored significant successes at Monza, where they gained the first three places and the Spanish Grand Prix at San Sebastian where they were first and second.

During the next three seasons Grand Prix racing was run on an entirely *Formule Libre* basis subject to only two stipulations – that two-seater bodies should be fitted and that races should not be of shorter duration than ten hours. The latter requirement turned Grands Prix into very stiff endurance as well as speed tests and necessitated the use of two drivers. Further new models made their appearance in 1931, including the first new Grand Prix Bugatti for several years, although in 1930 a 16-cylinder design had been entered in speed trials and hill climbs. [figure 15]. The engine consisted of two 8-cylinder blocks similar to the Type 35 mounted side by side on a common crankcase but each having its own rear-mounted supercharger. The capacity was 3,801 cc (60 × 84 mm) and 250 bhp was developed at 5,700 rpm.

The new Grand Prix car was the Type 51, which differed little in chassis design from the 35 but was the first competition Bugatti to feature twin overhead camshafts. The

17 Louis Chiron with the 4·9-litre Type 54 Bugatti. These cars were very fast but handled badly.

capacity was 2,261 cc (60 × 100 mm), the eight cylinders were cast in one block with a fixed head and 187 bhp was developed. The Type 51 cylinder head layout was very similar to that of the front-wheel-drive Miller, and it has often been said that Bugatti gained his inspiration for this layout from the cars he acquired from the American driver Leon Duray, who had found himself in financial difficulties after racing at Monza in 1929. The Type 51 was also produced in 1·5- and 2-litre forms and in all about forty of these cars were built.

1931 also saw the appearance of the Type 54 Bugatti [figure 17] at the Monza Grand Prix in September. This was intended for use primarily on the faster circuits and was hastily produced to provide some opposition at Monza for the twin-engined Alfa Romeos and Maseratis. The engine was a 'hotted-up' version of the 8-cylinder Type 50 touring car unit. The capacity was 4,972 cc (86 × 107 mm) and 300 bhp was developed at 4,500 rpm. This engine was also used to power an unsuccessful four-wheel-drive car which appeared the following year. The main reason for its failure was Bugatti's inability to appreciate the necessity for the use of constant velocity joints. It did, how-ever, have the distinction of being the only Bugatti to have independent front suspension. The chassis of the Types 51, 54 and the 16-cylinder car were similar apart from their dimensions, but the Type 54 had a gearbox with only three speeds. During three seasons of spasmodic racing appearances the Type 54 gained only two major successes, the Avusrennen and the British Empire Trophy in 1933.

A remarkably high number of new racing cars were introduced in 1931 and Alfa Romeo designer Vittorio Jano contributed two. The first of these was the legendary 8c Monza [figure 29], so named after its victory in the 1931 Italian Grand Prix at Monza. The 8C had first appeared in sports car form in the Mille Miglia that year, and indeed the Monza racing car was quite suitable for use in sports car events. In design it had much in common with the 6-cylinder Alfa production sports cars of the period and also with the later Monoposto Grand Prix car. The engine was an 8-cylinder design with the cylinders cast in two blocks of four and the train of gears driving the twin overhead camshafts mounted between them. The same cylinder dimensions as for the 1750 sports car were used, 65 × 88 mm, which gave a capacity of 2,336 cc. Both the cylinder blocks and the one piece head were of alloy, dry sump lubrication was featured and in Monza form 178 bhp was developed at 5,400 rpm. Transmission was by a multi-plate clutch and 4-speed gearbox and the channel-section chassis had semi-elliptic springs front and rear.

In addition to the Monza a further new Alfa made its debut in the 1931 Italian Grand Pix. This was the Tipo 'A', a follower in the vogue of using two engines, in this instance from Alfa's production 1750 sports cars. These 6-cylinder 65 × 88 mm units were geared together, but with the crankshafts revolving in opposite directions and the exhaust ports on the left and right-hand sides of the engine. There was a separate clutch, gearbox, prop-shaft and differential for each engine, and each of the differentials drove a different wheel. There were separate gear levers linked together and both clutches were operated by a single pedal. Unlike the Monza, which won the Italian Grand Prix and enjoyed a long and successful career, the Tipo 'A' crashed in practice for this race, killing the driver, Arcangeli, and in all appeared only three times. It was driven in the Italian race by Nuvolari, but was withdrawn, and then scored a surprising win in the Coppa Acerbo at Pescara. Finally two Tipo 'A' cars ran, but retired, in the Monza Grand Prix.

18 The straight-eight engine of the Alfa Romeo Monza. Note the beautifully ribbed inlet manifolding.

19 The Monoposto Alfa Romeo, so known because of its single-seater body, was a direct development from the Monza.

20 The straight engine of the Monoposto seen from the exhaust side.

There appeared at the Monza Grand Prix a further new model from Maserati, the 8C-2800, which was simply the earlier 2½-litre car with an enlarged engine of 2,795 cc (68 × 94 mm) and a power output of 198 bhp at 6,000 rpm. The Maserati team was still not sufficiently strong in numbers of organization to be a serious force in Grand Prix racing and neither the 8C-2800 nor the Alfa Romeo Monza, which was basically a sports car, were a real match for the Bugatti Type 51 which took the lion's share of Grand Prix honours in 1931. To rectify this situation Vittorio Jano used the vast experience he had gained in designing the P2, the 1750 sports and the Monza to produce in 1932 a car that was more than a match for anything racing at that time.

Perhaps the lines of the new Alfa Romeo Monoposto [figure 19] did not match the Gallic splendour of the Type 59 Bugatti which appeared the following year; perhaps there was not the same flair for mechanical artistry; but nevertheless the Monoposto was one of the best looking and best performing Grand Prix cars of pre-war years. The Monoposto resembled the Monza in both design and construction. Again an in-line 8-cylinder engine was favoured, but capacity was 2,654 cc (the stroke had been increased from 88 to 100 mm) and there were two small superchargers and two carburetters. Power output was 198 bhp at 5,400 rpm. In one respect, however, the design of the Monoposto was unique, for it had twin propellor shafts, enclosed in torque tubes and leading from a single differential immediately to the rear of the gearbox at an angle of thirty degrees. It was clear that this layout had been inspired by the earlier twin-engined Tipo 'A', but it was not so clear what the technical advantages were. There was a certain reduction in un-sprung weight, but the driver was seated above the prop-shafts, thereby increasing the overall height, whereas later designers offset the prop shaft, allowing drivers to sit alongside it. For 1932 the minimum race distance was reduced to five hours and single-seater bodywork was permitted, so the body of the Monoposto was purely of chassis width.

During 1932 Monopostos demonstrated their superiority over the Bugatti and Maserati by winning six out of eight events entered. For 1933 Alfa Romeo withdrew from racing for financial reasons, and Scuderia Ferrari, who had been racing Alfas on behalf of the works since the 1930 season, were forced to bring out the Monzas from under their dust-sheets. Despite an increase in capacity to 2,557 cc by boring out to 68 mm, these were no match for the new Maserati in the 1933 season.

The new Maserati was a 2,991 cc (69 × 100 mm) version of the 8C-2800 with a power output of 220 bhp at 5,500 rpm and a

21 (*below left*) The cockpit of a Monoposto. Note the twin tachometers which were standard on these cars.

22 (*right*) Power and Fury – Ken Hutchison's Monoposto with Dubonnet front suspension and fitted with twin rear wheels for hill climbing. The car is seen at Shelsley Walsh Hill Climb in 1948.

maximum speed of around 155 mph. After the first three cars had been built as the 8C-3000 with two-seater bodywork, Maserati turned out the 8CM-3000 with a single-seater body. Certainly the Monza Alfa was no match for the new Maserati, especially after Nuvolari had joined the Maserati team in mid-season. After he had won the Coppa Ciano at Montenero by over eight minutes from the Alfa Romeo Monza in second place, the Alfa factory felt forced to release the Monopostos again to Scuderia Ferrari. The result was that Monopostos won four races in a row, including the Italian Grand Prix, and subsequently scored wins in the Czechoslovakian and Spanish events.

23 Rear view of a Monoposto with reversed quarter-elliptic rear suspension.

The Spanish Grand Prix in September saw the appearance of a new Bugatti model, the Type 59 [figure 34], which took fourth and sixth places in the hands of Varzi and Dreyfus. The Type 59 had been built with the forthcoming 750 kg Formula in mind and in its original form had a straight-eight engine of 2,821 cc (67 × 100 mm). After the 1934 Monaco Grand Prix, however, the capacity of the engine was increased to 3,257 cc (72 × 100 mm), the same as for the Type 57 production model which it closely resembled. The Type 59 engine had twin overhead camshafts driven from the rear, a crankshaft running in nine plain bearings, a Roots-type supercharger and twin Zenith carburettors. The chassis was a typical Molsheim product, tapering from 9-inch depth at the centre to 2-inch at the front and sweeping upwards over the rear axle. It was much drilled to reduce weight and had semi-elliptic suspension at the front and the usual Bugatti reversed quarter-elliptic springs at the rear. The wire wheels were unique in that serrations on the inner edge of the rims corresponded with serrations on the edge of the brake drums and the assembly was supported by two rows of fine gauge spokes. The body was constructed from elektron.

Another racing marque to appear at this time was the Nacional Pescara, [figure 12], a competition-tuned version of a 2·8-litre straight-eight touring car built in Barcelona. The competition cars had a 3-litre engine of 72·2 × 90 mm, twin gear-driven overhead camshafts and an aluminium cylinder head. Power output was a modest 110 bhp at 5,000 rpm and transmission was by a 3-speed gearbox. In 1931 the make won the racing car class of the European Mountain (Hill Climb) Championship. After appearing again in hill climbs in 1933 the Spanish driver Esteban Tort drove one of the cars in the 1934-5 Penya Rhin Grands Prix.

From 1931 to 1933 racing was fought out between three major teams, Alfa Romeo, Bugatti and Maserati, but none of these was to figure prominently in racing events of the next few years. Representatives of all three makes have survived and examples of the Alfa Romeo Monoposto, the Types 51 and 59 Bugattis and the 8CM-3000 Maseratis can all be seen from time to time in Historic Racing events (there is now more than one Monoposto in the U.K.).

24 The 8C-3000 Maserati, driven here by the Hon. Brian Lewis in the 1934 International Trophy at Brooklands.

Overleaf

25 (*left*) The Type 37 Bugatti used the 'Brescia' 4-cylinder engine and was intended for use by private owners. This car is seen taking part in a British Hill Climb in 1965.

26 (*top right*) The Delage 1½-litre was the most successful racing car of the years 1926-7, and one in rebuilt form achieved equal success in the thirties in the hands of Dick Seaman. Here the rebuilt car is seen in an early post-war race at Silverstone.

27 (*bottom right*) The Sunbeam 4-litre used by Segrave to break the World's Land Speed Record and in various racing events. The car has now been restored to its original red finish.

25

CHAPTER THREE

The Years of Power

FOR six tumultuous years Grand Prix racing was dominated by the German Auto Union and Mercedes-Benz teams and racing provided a spectacle of speed, sound and fury never previously attained and never since matched. After several years of unsuccessful Formulae that failed to achieve any effective control over the type of cars raced, the Association Internationale des Automobile Clubs Reconnus, the then controlling body of international motor sport, announced in late 1932 a new Formula for the years 1934-6 (subsequently extended to 1937) that was intended to rationalize rather than revolutionize racing. The principal stipulation was that dry weight (that is, without fuel, water, oil, tyres or driver) should not exceed 750 kilogrammes (14·73 cwt). It was considered that this would restrict entries to cars of a similar type to the 2·6-litre Monoposto Alfa Romeo and the 2·3-litre Type 51 Bugatti. The very fast cars, such as the 16-cylinder 5-litre *Sedici Cilindri* Maserati and the 12-cylinder 3½-litre Tipo 'A' Alfa Romeo, both twin-engined, weighed rather more than 750 kg. The other requirements of the new Formula were that the cross-sectional area of the bodywork at the driving seat should not be less than 85×25 cm and that all races should be run over a minimum distance of 500 kilometres (310 miles).

As far as the existing contenders were concerned, the new Formula would probably have worked, as, at the beginning of 1934, Maserati were ready to continue racing their 3-litre 8-cylinder car and Alfa Romeo continued to race the Monoposto, now with an engine of 2,905 cc (68×100 mm) developing

28 (*opposite*) Ettore Bugatti made a half-hearted return to Grand Prix racing in 1938 with a straight-eight 3-litre car seen here on its debut at Cork.

Overleaf
29 (*left*) A superbly restored example of the Alfa Romeo Monza. These cars first appeared in 1931 and were used in both sports and racing car events.

30 (*right*) The straight engine of the Monoposto

215 bhp at 5,400 rpm, a widened cockpit and known for the first time as the Tipo 'B'. Bugatti raced the Type 59 with a 3,257 cc (72 × 100 mm) engine developing 240 bhp. The Bugatti engine was further enlarged to 3·8-litres in 1935. Although outclassed by the German cars, a Type 59 won the 1934 Belgian Grand Prix, and it was the most beautifully constructed of all Grand Prix cars. There were, however, to be two new contenders, Mercedes-Benz, who had last built a pure racing car in 1926, and Auto Union. Together, they were to apply such a completely new and scientific approach to motor racing that not only were the aims of the new Formula thrown overboard, but all other entrants were outclassed.

The Auto Union, or 'P-wagen', as it was originally known, was designed by Dr Ferdinand Porsche for the group formed by the amalgamation of the DKW, Horch, Wanderer and Audi Companies. The Auto Union [figure 31] was the first successful rear-engined Grand Prix car, but not the first rear-engined car of its type, which had been the 'tear-drop' Benz 2-litre car based on a design by Dr Rumpler and raced during 1923. The idea behind the new Mercedes and Auto Union designs was to use as powerful an engine as possible without exceeding the weight restriction. The Auto Union had a v-16 4,360 cc (68 × 75 mm) engine with the two banks of cylinders set at an angle of forty-five degrees and the valves actuated by a single overhead camshaft. With a Roots-type supercharger compressing at 9 lb psi and twin Solex carburetters, power output was approximately 295 bhp at 4,500 rpm. The engine was mounted immediately ahead of the rear axle and was directly coupled to the unit 5-speed gearbox and final drive. Several features were common to both German designs, including an exceptionally stiff chassis, independent suspension front and rear, hydraulic brakes and an aerodynamically efficient body. The Auto Union had the now classic independent front suspension by which each wheel was carried on two trailing arms connected to transverse torsion bars. At the rear there was a swing-axle layout, with a single transverse leaf spring mounted above the rear axle and radius arms running from the ends of the half-axles to the frame side-members. The radiator

was mounted conventionally at the front, and the two hefty parallel side-members served also to carry the water to and from the engine. Between the engine and the radiator sat the driver, his feet extending to just beyond the front hubs, and immediately behind was a 48-gallon fuel tank. The first model, known as the Type A, had an unladen weight of 1,556 lb, which was comfortably within the 750 kg (1,649 lb) limit. In appearance the Auto Union looked low and rather squat, with a large, half-oval radiator grille, a long tapering tail and a short exhaust on either side.

Dr Porsche's main arguments in favour of the rear-mounting of the engine were that, unlike cars of conventional layout with the fuel tank mounted in the tail, the car's handling did not change as the fuel was used up, and that power losses through the transmission were lower. He did not, however, take fully into account the fact that the driver, seated at the front, became aware far later of sliding action of the tail and that exceptional sensitivity and reactions were needed to deal with this.

Dr Hans Nibel and Herr Wagner, who were responsible for the design of the Mercedes-Benz w.25 [figure 32], had both been with the company when the rear-engined *Tropfenwagen* was being raced and they were well aware of the merits – and the drawbacks – of this layout. It was, therefore, only after very lengthy consideration that the rear-engined layout was rejected, but in all other respects the design of the Mercedes was as advanced as that of the Auto Union. Independent suspension was still something of an innovation on racing cars, and the system used on the Mercedes was particularly well thought out. An exceptionally stiff chassis of box-section steel

31 (*left*) A new contender in Grand Prix racing was the Auto Union with a rear-mounted V-16 4·36-litre engine.

32 (*right*) In 1934 Mercedes-Benz re-entered Grand Prix racing with the W.25 model powered by a 3·36-litre straight-eight engine.

Overleaf
33 (*left*) At first Maserati also raced an existing model, the 8CM-3000, but not unexpectedly it was no match for its German rivals.

34 (*right*) The 3·3-litre Bugatti Type 59 was one of the most beautifully constructed racing cars of all time.

35 During the first two years of the new Formula, Alfa Romeo continued to race the Monoposto. Varzi's car is seen leading a Bugatti in the 1934 Monaco Grand Prix.

construction was used with, at the front, double wishbones of almost equal length and coil springs and, at the rear, a system of swing axles. With this system, each wheel was mounted on a tubular half-axle containing the drive-shafts and with a short leaf spring-anchored to the frame at the inner end and to the extremity of the half-axle at the outer. Hydraulic brakes were fitted and the gearbox was in unit with the final drive.

Following previous Mercedes practice, the engine was an in-line 8-cylinder unit, with a capacity of 3,360 cc (78 × 88 mm) and twin overhead camshafts. The cylinders were separate castings surrounded by a welded steel water jacket and the crankshaft ran in roller main bearings. With a large double-rotor supercharger mounted vertically at the front of the engine and twin carburetters, 354 bhp was developed at 5,800 rpm. The body was a well-streamlined single-seater with a cowling over the radiator and front suspension and was constructed from thin-gauge light alloy.

At the beginning of the 1934 season the German cars were not yet ready to race and the early events continued to be dominated by the Scuderia Ferrari Monopostos. The Auto Unions made their debut in the very fast Avusrennen track race, but were delayed by mechanical troubles and victory went to the special Tipo 'B' 3.2-litre Alfa driven by Guy Moll and fitted

36 There appeared at the 1934 Italian Grand Prix a new 6-cylinder 3·3-litre Maserati, the Tipo 34. Tazio Nuvolari is at the wheel.

with a bulbous streamlined body designed by Ing. Pallavicino. Mercedes-Benz won the Eifelrennen at the Nürburgring on their debut, but although the Alfa Romeos and Maseratis were out-classed by the German cars in terms of both speed and road-holding, they were able to benefit from the teething troubles of their rivals and there were also events in which the German cars were not entered. Scuderia Ferrari Alfas won the French Grand Prix, while Auto Union took the Swiss race and Mercedes were the winners at the German, Italian and Spanish events.

The Italian race saw the debut of the first new Italian car since the commencement of the 750 kg Formula. This was the Maserati Tipo 34 [figure 36], a combination of the existing 8CM-3000 chassis with a new 6-cylinder twin overhead camshaft 3,326 cc (84 × 100 mm) engine developing 260 bhp. The engine had been under development for some while, and from the moment the Mercedes and Auto Union appeared, the Maserati brothers realised the futility of proceeding with this Grand Prix project and it became purely a 'stop-gap' pending the appear-ance of a more advanced car in 1935. The 8-cylinder Maseratis only just complied with the 750 kg weight limit and it became apparent at Monza that the Tipo 34 was no lighter than its predecessors. At the weighing-in, even the hydraulic fluid for the brakes was drained off, and the mechanics forgot to top up

Overleaf
37 The 1937 Auto Union driven in the Swiss Grand Prix by Bernd Rosemeyer.

the reserve reservoir afterwards. As a result the Tipo 34, driven by Nuvolari, ran completely out of brakes and he was forced to slow the car on the gearbox. Later in the year, Nuvolari won two minor events, the Circuits of Modena and Naples, with the Tipo 34, but in general neither this original car nor the 3,729 cc version which appeared in 1935 achieved a great deal of success.

Hitler had offered an award of 500,000 *Reichmarks* (equivalent to about £42,000 or $100,800) for the most successful German car to race under the new Formula, and this was shared between Auto Union and Mercedes-Benz, but it fell far short of the sums expended by the two companies on developing and racing their cars. There was some dissension among the Auto Union directors, as Direktor Werner was convinced that the rear-engined layout was inherently wrong, but thought that any radical change would bring the Company adverse publicity. Dr Porsche was equally convinced that his design was right, and as he was supported by Professor Eberan von Eberhorst, head of the racing engine department, the layout remained unchanged. Engine capacity, however, was increased to 4,950 cc (72 × 75 mm) and power rose to 375 bhp at 4,700 rpm. Torsion bars replaced the transverse leaf spring at the rear and there were now separate water pipes, as the tubular side-members tended to leak. The 1935 car was known as the Type 'B' to distinguish it from its predecessor.

Mercedes-Benz changes were limited to increasing the stroke, with a new crankshaft, to 94·5 mm, thereby raising the capacity to 3,990 cc, and power output rose to 430 bhp. During the 1935 season the stroke was further increased to 102 mm, giving a capacity of 4,310 cc and power output was 495 bhp. The Company also pioneered the use of the limited slip differential by fitting one of ZF manufacture, which permitted one wheel to spin 15 per cent more than the other before a system of wedge-shaped cams running freely between rotating sleeves jammed solid, and locked the differential.

During the winter of 1934–5, frantic efforts to produce competitive Grand Prix cars were being made both in Italy and France, but no new cars were ready for the beginning of the 1935 season. At the Monaco Grand Prix in April, the first important race, as well as the enlarged 3·7-litre Maseratis there was a 2·9-litre 8-cylinder Maserati with the engine bored out to 3·2-litres and independent front suspension by torsion bars running parallel to the frame which was driven by Goffredo Zehender, and modified versions of the Tipo 'B' Alfa Romeos entered by Scuderia Ferrari. These had 3,160 cc (78 × 100 mm) engines, 3- (instead of 4-) speed gearboxes, Dubonnet front suspension, which incorporated trailing links steered with the wheels and mounted on the end of a tubular axle, and Ariston hydraulic brakes made by the Farina coachbuilding firm. Mercedes, however, won at Monaco and repeated this success in the Tripoli Grand Prix and the Avusrennen in May. In both these later races the Germans were faced with formidable, almost terrifying opposition from two Scuderia Ferrari entries. These were the notorious *Bi-motore* Alfas designed for the team by Luigi Bazzi. The standard Monoposto chassis was lengthened, with one engine in the normal position and the other at the rear in the triangle formed by the two propellor shafts and the rear axle. The driver sat on the gearbox between the two engines. One of these cars had a total capacity of 6·4 litres and the other of 5·8 litres. The cars weighed well over the 750 kg limit and could therefore run only in *Formule Libre* events. Maximum speed was close to 200 mph, the handling was so bad as to scare the most courageous of drivers and the cars had such a voracious appetite for tyres that pit stops ruined their chances of winning. One was sold to Austin Dobson, who raced it with trailing link front suspension before it was acquired by Max Aitken. Aitken rebuilt the car with a single engine at the front and this was raced in post-war days with the engine enlarged to 3·4-litres by Tony Rolt. This car is now in New Zealand.

In France, Ettore Bugatti had produced a revised version of the Type 59, known as the 50B, with a 4,700 cc (84 × 107 mm) engine, central driving position and fairly well streamlined bodywork. No serious attempts were made to race either this or the SEFAC (Société des Etudes Francaises d'Automobiles de Course), another French car designed by Emil Petit, who had been responsible for the 8-cylinder Amilcar raced in the twenties. The engine of the SEFAC was a 2,970 cc (70 × 90 mm) 8-cylinder unit with two blocks of four cylinders mounted side by side and two crankshafts geared together, one driving a supercharger and the other coupled directly to a 4-speed gearbox. Coil spring suspension was used front and rear and there were six shoes in each brake drum, although they were operated by a rather primitive cable system.

Maserati, in the meantime, had been developing a car that in many ways aped the Mercedes concept. This was the Tipo V8-R1 with a stiff channel-section frame electrically welded up by a special American process, independent front suspension by double wishbones and torsion bars and independent rear suspension by swing axles and semi-elliptic springs. The engine was a V-8 of 4·4 litres, developing 320 bhp. Although this was increased to 4,785 cc for 1936, the V8-R1 proved to be uncompetitive and unreliable, and as the Maserati brothers were concentrating on the development of the 6CM voiturette, they had little enthusiasm for making the Grand Prix car a raceworthy proposition. Another Italian project which, in this case, was never raced, was the car designed by Count Trossi, one-time President of Scuderia Ferrari. This had a chassis constructed on similar lines to that of an aircraft fuselage and independent suspension on all four wheels. The power unit was a 16-cylinder supercharged radial air-cooled two-stroke design of 3,926 cc (65 × 74 mm) mounted ahead of the front wheels which it drove through a directly-coupled gearbox/differential unit.

The 1935 season was completely dominated by Mercedes-Benz, even the Auto Unions being overshadowed. The sole Auto Union successes during the year were in the Coppa Acerbo at Pescara, the Masaryk Grand Prix, which Mercedes did not enter, and the Italian Grand Prix where the entire Mercedes team retired. The sensation of the year, however, was the German Grand Prix, in which Nuvolari drove the outdated Monoposto. Certain of these cars now had 3,822 cc (78 × 100 mm) engines, but even so suffered from a deficiency

38 (above) As successor to the Monoposto, Alfa Romeo introduced in 1935 the 8C-35 using the same engine. Dennis Poore won with it the 1950 Hill Climb Championship.

42

39 (*below*) Farina at the wheel of a 12C-312 3-litre Alfa Romeo in practice for the 1938 Swiss Grand Prix. The chassis was basically that of the earlier 12C-36.

of some 60 bhp compared with Mercedes-Benz. On the difficult and long Nürburgring, where roadholding and driving were still at a premium, Nuvolari, aided by a wet road and the fact that the two leading Mercedes drivers were off form, defeated all the German cars, winning from Stuck's Auto Union by over two minutes.

The Italian Grand Prix had seen the appearance of another Italian contender, from Alfa Romeo. This was the 8C-35 [figure 38], a completely new chassis using the existing Monoposto engine in its 3·8-litre form. Once again the German influence was evident and the channel-section frame had independent suspension at the front by trailing links and coil springs enclosing hydraulic dampers and independent suspension at the rear by swing-axles and a transverse leaf spring. Hydraulic brakes were fitted and the gearbox was in unit with the rear axle. The body style was much in advance of previous Alfa practice. Scuderia Ferrari raced 8C-35s throughout 1936 and Nuvolari succeeded in beating the German teams with one of these cars in the Hungarian Grand Prix, the Circuit of Milan and the Coppa Ciano at Leghorn. By 1937 Ferrari was racing only the 12C-36 [figure 39], which consisted of the 8C-35 with the engine primarily intended for it, a V-12 of 4,064 cc (70 × 88 mm) with twin overhead camshafts per bank of cylinders and developing 360 bhp at 5,800 rpm. This was the last racing Alfa Romeo to be designed by Vittorio Jano before he left to join the Lancia Company. An 8C-35 was sold to the Swiss driver Hans Ruesch, and this was acquired in 1947 by Dennis Poore. Poore used the car consistently in British races and, despite its basic unsuitability for this type of event, succeeded in winning the 1950 RAC Hill Climb Championship.

For 1936 Dr Porsche increased the capacity of the Auto Union to 6,006 cc (75 × 85 mm), which gave it a power output of 520 bhp at 5,000 rpm. In this form the Auto Union had a maximum speed of close to 195 mph and was known as the Type 'C'. Mercedes-Benz, however, carried out more drastic modifications to their design and produced the ostensibly much improved Type W25E with a 4,740 cc (86 × 102 mm) engine developing 480 bhp at 5,800 rpm. The substantial increase in power output was offset by inferior steering, roadholding and the inability to transmit to the road as much of the power as was desirable. Apart from wins by Mercedes early in the season at Monaco and Carthage (the Tunis Grand Prix), the season was very much an Auto Union benefit, and of twelve races entered by the team they won six, losing the remaining four to Nuvolari's Alfa, defeated not by superior cars, but by the little Mantuan's unmatchable driving skill.

Content with the performance of their cars, Auto Union made few changes for 1937 and were content with introducing two-leading-shoe brakes and modified steering. At Stuttgart, work had been going on on a new and much improved car, the W125 [figure 41], originally intended for use with a 3-litre engine, but fitted with a straight-eight 5,660 cc (94 × 102 mm) twin overhead camshaft engine, developing a colossal 645 bhp at 5,800 rpm and making it capable of attaining 200 mph. The W125 had an extremely light tubular chassis constructed from nickel chrome molybdenum steel, a revised system of front suspension by long wishbones and exposed vertical coil springs, and a completely radical rear suspension. This was a resurrection of the de Dion system, which had lain dormant for almost forty years. With this system the wheels were located by a dead tube attached to the hubs and driven through two universal joints by open shafts from a bevel box mounted on the frame.

By 1937, Alfa's participation in Grand Prix racing was indeed half-hearted, and the appearance of a new low-chassis version of the 12C with a 4,500 cc (72 × 92 mm) engine developing 480 bhp at 5,800 rpm was a token effort. Although Alfas won a few minor events in home territory, the major races were largely dominated by the new Mercedes-Benz, which won the Tripoli, German, Monaco, Swiss, Italian and Masaryk races. Auto Unions driven by the brilliant Bernd Rosemeyer succeeded in gaining victories in the Eifelrennen at the Nürburgring, the Vanderbilt Cup on Long Island in the United States, the Coppa Acerbo and the Donington race. The young Rudi Hasse scored a brilliant win for Auto Union in the Belgian Grand Prix. The Donington race was the last of the 750 kg For-

40 The cockpit of the 1937 Mercedes. Note the right-hand gear-change and the tachometer running up to 7000 rpm.

41 (*right*) The 1937 Grand Prix Mercedes, the W.125 with a 6-litre engine developing 646 bhp at 5800 rpm.

mula, and the last in which Rosemeyer ever drove, for he was killed in January 1938 during a record attempt on the Frankfurt Autobahn. For record-breaking, Mercedes had produced a special car known as the W125/DAB with a V-12 engine of 5,570 cc (82 × 88 mm) and developing 736 bhp at 6,000 rpm. The cars had highly streamlined bodywork and were also run in the *Formule Libre* Avusrennen, a race held on a banked circuit near Berlin. During this race Rosemeyer set a lap record of 171·6 mph and the event was won by Lang's Mercedes at an average of 162·5 mph, the highest race average recorded until the 1958 Monza 500 mile event which was won at 166·72 mph.

During the four years of the 750 kg Formula considerable technical advances had been achieved in Grand Prix racing. Coil spring and torsion bar suspension had almost completely super-seded the traditional leaf spring layout, hydraulic brakes had become universal and power outputs had risen in absolute terms from the 215 bhp of the 1934 Monoposto Alfa to the 646 bhp of the W125 Mercedes, or, in comparative terms, from 72 bhp/litre to 110-bhp/litre. By this stage, engines were becoming too powerful for their chassis and, with a view to limiting lap speeds and to encouraging other manufacturers to enter racing, a new Formula was introduced for the years 1938-40. This restricted weights in accordance with capacity on a sliding scale from 666 cc up to a maximum of 3,000 cc supercharged and 4,500 cc unsupercharged. The minimum weight for the larger capacity cars was 850 kg and, in all cases, there was a minimum body width of 85 cm. The weight reduction for small capacity cars, however, did not offer any real advantages.

Now that Dr Porsche was fully engaged on the Volkswagen project, Auto Union development was conducted by Direktor Werner, and the Chemnitz team chose a 2,990 cc (65 × 75 mm) V-12 engine with two banks of cylinders set at an angle of sixty degrees, a central camshaft actuating the inlet valves, and two outer camshafts, driven by shafts and bevel gears from the centre camshaft, operating the exhaust valves. A single vertical Roots-type supercharger was retained and power output of the D-type was 400 bhp at 7,000 rpm. The chassis was very similar to that of the early cars, but, following Mercedes practice, a de Dion axle had now been adopted with the tube located by a transverse Panhard rod. The driver now sat further to the rear of the car and thus had a better indication of when the limit of adhesion had been reached.

Mercedes' contribution to the new Formula was the W154 [figure 42], which used a chassis almost identical to that of the 1937 cars, but the engine was a new 2,960 cc (67 × 70 mm) V-12 with twin overhead camshafts per bank of cylinders, four valves per cylinder and welded steel water jackets. With twin Roots-type superchargers the power output was 420 bhp at the very high crankshaft speed of 7,800 rpm. This engine was derived from that of the record-breaking cars referred to earlier. An innovation was the mounting of the engine at an angle to the centre line of the chassis and tilted downwards slightly at the rear, enabling the prop-shaft to run alongside the driver's seat, which was correspondingly lower. As this engine was averaging 3 mpg under racing conditions, to avoid increasing the number of pit stops fuel tankage was increased to 88 gallons and a control was provided for the driver to alter the setting of the rear dampers so as to counteract the variation in weight.

43 The 1939 3-litre Mercedes had a restyled frontal treatment and even smoother lines. Note particularly the large ribbed brake drums with gauze-covered ventilators.

42 (*left*) This view of the W.154 Mercedes emphasises its aerodynamically clean and very efficient shape.

The former leaders of Grand Prix racing, Alfa Romeo, Maserati and Bugatti, all made half-hearted contributions to the racing scene. Alfa's contribution was one chassis with a total of three different engines. This was known in its original form as the 8C-308 with a 2,994 cc (69 × 100 mm) version of the old Monoposto engine developing 295 bhp at 6,000 rpm and was similar in most respects to the tubular 12C-37 chassis of the previous year. Alfa Romeo also developed a 12-cylinder model known as the 12C-312 with a 2,997 cc (66 × 73 mm) version of the 1937 4½-litre engine developing 320 bhp at 6,500 rpm. Neither of these engines was sufficiently powerful, and a 16-cylinder unit of 2,959 cc (58 × 70 mm) developing 350 bhp at 7,000 rpm was insufficiently developed to provide the German cars with serious opposition. It did, however, take fourth place in the 1939 Belgian race, the last Grand Prix which the works Alfa team, Alfa Corse, entered before the outbreak of war, and one half of it formed the basis of the Tipo 158 Alfa described in chapter five. Examples of the 8c-308 did pass into private ownership, but none are known to have survived.

44 The V-12 4½-litre Delahaye first appeared with two-seater bodywork, but the later version, seen here, was a normal single-seater.

Maserati's creation, the Tipo 8CTF, was based on the existing 4CM voiturette design and was purely a token effort. The engine was a straight eight of 2,992 cc formed from two 4-cylinder 69 × 100 mm blocks and developing 360 bhp at 6,500 rpm. The chassis was a simple, almost naïve structure with channel-section members, independent front suspension by wishbones and torsion bars and a live rear axle on semi-elliptic springs. The model's best European performance was third place in the 1939 German Grand Prix with Paul Pietsch at the wheel.

From France there were three contenders for the new Formula. Bugatti made a brief return to Grand Prix racing with the Type 60. This used the earlier Type 50B chassis with a 2,992 cc (78 × 78 mm) version of the same twin overhead camshaft engine. The 3-litre car made its debut in the 1938 Cork Grand Prix, where it was timed over a kilometre at 147·2 mph, but retired. In 1939 a similar car with the 4·7-litre Type 50B engine was built, but this was of course ineligible for Grand Prix racing and was used only in hill climbs. It did, however, win the first post-war race, the Coupe des Prisonniers, held in the Bois de Boulogne in Paris in September 1945. The

Delahaye factory produced an interesting car with a V-12 4,490 cc (75 × 84·7 mm) engine developing 245 bhp and a de Dion rear axle. This was a reliable but not very fast car made in both single- and two-seater forms, and among its successes were wins in the 1938 Pau and Cork Grands Prix. During 1938, Antony Lago of the Lago-Talbot concern raced his sports two-seaters in certain Grands Prix, but a single-seater version ran in the 1939 French Grand Prix. These cars originally featured a 3,996 cc pushrod 6-cylinder engine, but a 4½-litre version appeared in 1938. They were much more successful in their fully redeveloped 4½-litre form of post-war years.

Auto Union development was slow, and the cars were not ready until the 1938 French Grand Prix in July, by which time Mercedes had chalked up a win at Tripoli, but had been defeated at Pau by Dreyfus's Delahaye, which ran through the race non-stop. Mercedes won easily at Rheims and scored four further major victories before Nuvolari, tired of driving outclassed Alfas, became sufficiently familiar with his Auto Union to defeat the Mercedes in the Italian Grand Prix – a victory he repeated in the International Grand Prix at Donington Park. For

45 The 1939 French Grand Prix also saw the appearance of the first single-seater Talbot. It was driven by Raymond Mays and retired with a leaking fuel tank.

49

1939 Auto Union fitted twin-stage supercharging which boosted power output to 485 bhp at 7,000 rpm, while Mercedes, also by the use of twin stage blowers, increased their power output to 485 bhp at 8,000 rpm and continued to dominate Grand Prix racing in 1939. Mercedes-Benz also introduced in 1939 a 1½-litre car which swept the board in the Tripoli Grand Prix; further reference to this car is made in the next chapter.

The outbreak of war in September, however, brought international racing to a halt and marked the end of an era in motor racing which had seen unprecedented technical advances and powerful cars, an era from which surviving cars are few and memories are many. The Italians continued their own voiturette events until Italy entered the war in 1940 and these

46 The start of the 1939 French Grand Prix at Rheims. Leading are the Auto Unions of Nuvolari (No. 8) and Muller (No. 12).

voiturettes had long and successful post-war careers. Three-litre cars from Mercedes's well-stocked museum at Stuttgart ran in the 1951 Peron Cup races at Buenos Aires, but were defeated by Gonzalez's 2-litre supercharged Ferrari, and a 3-litre car found its way to America where it ran, without success, in the Indianapolis 500-mile race. After the war the original Auto Union factory was on the wrong side of the iron curtain, and the fate of the cars is unknown, apart from a C-type chassis on display in the Munich Deutsches-Museum and a car on exhibition in a Moscow technical institute.

Overshadowed by the German cars of breathtaking performance and developed at vast cost, the British racing cars of the thirties, many of which were built by enthusiasts of very limited means, are only too easy to forget. Notable among these were the ERA referred to in chapter five and the Alta which was the work of Geoffrey Taylor. All Altas were based on a 4-cylinder engine with twin roller-chain driven overhead camshafts, the cylinder and valve gear layout following that of the Norton racing motor-cycle engine. The 2-litre version developed a claimed 270 bhp and the 1937-8 1,496 cc (69 × 100 mm) version with independent suspension by coil springs and vertical slides formed a satisfactory ERA-chaser in British short circuit events.

47 The 12-cylinder 3-litre Auto Union of 1938 which had a power output of 500 bhp at 7000 rpm.

51

One of the most successful British cars of this era was the Multi-Union [figure 49] of test pilot Chris Staniland. This was based on a 2·9-litre Alfa Romeo Monoposto, but was progressively modified so that its relationship to the original was barely recognisable. By 1939 the modifications included an engine increased in capacity to 2,947 cc, a streamlined body reminiscent of the 1935 Mercedes, Técnauto independent front suspension by trailing links and coil springs, a new 4-speed gearbox and larger twin leading shoe hydraulic brakes with front and rear braking ratios which were adjustable from the cockpit. In 1939 the Multi-Union lapped Brooklands at 142·3 mph – running only on seven cylinders as a valve had fallen in. Staniland was killed during the war and the Multi-Union's engine suffered serious damage at the 1949 Brighton Speed Trials. The car survives, however, and it is hoped that it will one day appear in Historic Racing Car events. Another choice car of this period was the single-seater chain-driven Frazer Nash fitted with a single overhead camshaft 1½-litre engine and developed by the Company, but generally known as the Gough after its designer. In post-war tests the works twin supercharged engine developed 151 bhp at 5,250 rpm. One of the best surviving Frazer Nashes is that of A. J. Gibson, which was originally the property of the Hon. Peter Aitken and raced by him in British short circuit events.

48 (opposite) The start of the 1939 Tripoli Grand Prix, one of the most significant races of all time. The cars nearest the camera are the W.165 Mercedes-Benz of Lang and Caracciola. To their left is one of the 158 Alfa Romeos and behind is a 4CL Maserati. The streamlined car, No. 38, is the special-bodied Maserati of Luigi Villoresi which had a claimed maximum speed of 170 mph.

49 The Multi-Union, owned and driven by Chris Staniland, was a very successful rebuild of a 2·9-litre Monoposto Alfa Romeo formerly belonging to Raymond Sommer.

54

CHAPTER FOUR

Indianapolis

FORMS of racing of all sorts from European-style sports and Grand Prix road racing events to dirt-track racing have long been held in the United States, but no other form of racing has attracted the intense and enthusiastic following of the 500-mile race at Indianapolis, a name which in the United States is synonymous with motor racing. Although the Indianapolis track had been opened several years before, the brick-lined 2½-mile circuit with its four evenly curved and slightly banked corners did not achieve a great deal of popularity until the first 500-mile race in 1911. For the first two years of the Formula an engine capacity of 600 cubic inches (just under 10 litres) was used. With the exception of the winning Marmon [figure 51], driven by Ray Harroun, all the cars in the race carried riding mechanics, and to overcome his lack of rearward vision, Harroun used what is claimed to be the first ever rear-view mirror. This Marmon Wasp had a 6-cylinder 7¾-litre engine and both this and the 4-cylinder 7·9-litre National which won the race in 1912 are on display in the Indianapolis Motor Speedway Museum.

European cars, however, were breathing hard down the exhaust pipes of their American rivals: a Fiat took third place in the 1911 race and one was second the following year. In 1913 the French Peugeot concern turned up with two of their 1912 Grand Prix cars. These very advanced cars had been designed by the brilliant Swiss engineer Ernest Henry and featured a monobloc engine casting, four valves per cylinder and twin overhead camshafts. Already the Peugeots had a win in the

51 The first Indianapolis 500-mile race was in 1911 and the winner was this Marmon Wasp which is now on display in the Indianapolis Motor Museum.

50 (opposite) The 4·2-litre Meyer-Drake Offenhauser 4-cylinder twin overhead camshaft engine which has powered a vast number of Indianapolis winners.

55

52 At Indianapolis in 1914 victory went to a European car and driver – this Delage driven by René Thomas at an average of 82·47 mph.

53 (opposite) The 1938 Mercedes had a 3-litre V-12 engine with a power output of 476 bhp. Von Brauchitsch is seen here in the 1938 Swiss Grand Prix.

French Grand Prix to their credit and at Indianapolis Jules Goux scored a convincing victory over American Mercer and Stutz entries. For the race the capacity of the Peugeots was slightly reduced to 7·4- from 7·6-litres to comply with the new Indianapolis limit of 450 cubic inches capacity. The Peugeot success encouraged a further European invasion in 1914 by a team of cars under the management of W. F. Bradley, for many years Continental Correspondent of the *Autocar*. In addition to an Excelsior and a 3-litre Peugeot, the European team fielded two 6·2-litre Delages [figure 52], another successful design which had so nearly won the French Grand Prix at Amiens and had won the Grand Prix de France at Sarthe in 1913. Despite a pit stop to patch up a fractured exhaust with rags and wire, René Thomas won at 82·47 mph with a Delage from the Peugeot of Leon Duray. Throughout the war years European cars continued to dominate the Indianapolis scene and in 1915 victory went to a Mercedes-Benz of the type which had won the 1914 French Grand Prix, and which was driven at the brickyard by Ralph de Palma. Peugeots again won the race in 1916, when it was held over a distance of only 300 miles, and it was resumed in 1919 after a two-year break.

The direct result of this European invasion was the adoption of Peugeot and Mercedes-Benz design principles by American constructors; such engines were built by Chevrolet, Stutz and Duesenberg, while the Premier concern built an engine that was

such a close imitation of the Peugeot that the components were interchangeable. There was, however, another influence at work on designers, the very successful aero engines of Ettore Bugatti; when the first post-war 500-mile race was held in 1919 to a 300 cubic in. (4,917 cc) Formula, both the leading contenders had been manufacturing this under licence. The French Ballot entries, which were the work of Ernest Henry, were long-stroke straight-eights of 4,894 cc featuring twin overhead camshafts and four valves per cylinder; the American Duesenberg entries, however, were closer devotees of Bugatti practice and, as well as adopting the straight-eight layout, had a single overhead camshaft, but operating one inlet and two exhaust valves per cylinder (the Bugatti engine featured two inlet and one exhaust valve per cylinder). The fortunes of racing are such that neither make won the race and victory went to a 1914 Peugeot driven by Howdy Wilcox, with a similar car in third place.

Domination of the race by European cars began to wane after this, but many still made the journey across the Atlantic to compete. In 1922 a solitary works Bentley appeared, not with any hope of winning the race, but as a demonstration of reliability by a stripped production sports car. This was driven by D. Hawkes and finished thirteenth at an average speed of 80 mph. The 1922 race was won by a Duesenberg driven by Jimmy Murphy, the same driver and car combination which had scored a brilliant victory in the 1921 French Grand Prix. For this race, however, the Duesenberg had been fitted with a Miller straight-eight engine, and it was undoubtedly the use of this engine that set Harry A. Miller on the road to fame. Miller was very much a devotee of the design principles laid down by Ernest Henry and embodied in the so successful Peugeots, but his war-time experience with the Bugatti aero engine led him to choose the straight-eight layout. The Miller engine had cylinder dimensions of 68·2 × 100·6 mm, twin overhead camshafts driven by a spur gear train in accordance with Peugeot practice, four valves per cylinder and a power output of approximately 125 bhp at 4,000 rpm.

For the years 1923-5 the Indianapolis race was run to a 2-litre Formula; not only did Miller build a batch of 59·5 × 89 mm engines to suit this, but, having perfected his basic engine design, he now also produced the cars in which to install the engines. Miller cars became renowned for their superb construction and the fine proportions of their components. Harry Miller himself became obsessed with reducing weight and all his cars were kept as light as possible. As well as scoring a victory in the 1923 Indianapolis race, Millers raced in all the other forms of speedway racing held throughout the country on boards, dirt and asphalt. During the early twenties the Duesenberg brothers had been carrying out many experiments with centrifugal supercharging and by leading in this field they snatched victory from the Millers in 1924; although two of the three Millers entered next year were supercharged, the Duesenbergs again won the 500-mile race, if only by the narrowest of margins.

While Alvis were developing front-wheel-drive racing and sports cars in Britain – the first cars appeared in 1925 – Miller was following similar lines of development. He built the first front-wheel-drive car in 1924 for Jimmy Murphy, who was killed before he could take delivery. What singled out the Miller from other front-wheel-drive designs was the use of the de Dion axle at the front suspended on double quarter-elliptic springs. The engine was reversed in the chassis so that the flywheel and clutch were at the front with the gearbox ahead of them. It was one of these cars driven by Lewis and Hill which took second place in the 1925 Indianapolis race, and Miller's front-wheel-drive system and inboard-mounted brake layout were adopted on the production Cord L29 model. Miller, however, also continued to build his more conventional rear-wheel-drive cars.

Keeping in step with Europe, a 1½-litre capacity limit was put into force for the year 1926, but remained at Indianapolis until 1929. Miller produced the classic '91' model with dimensions of 55.5×76.2 mm. In its original form this developed 154 bhp, but with development work and running on alcohol this was subsequently increased to a little over 250 bhp at 8,000 rpm. This model, driven by Frank Lockhart, won the Indianapolis race in 1926, when rain reduced the distance to 400 miles. The following year Lockhart gained further fame for the make by clocking 171 mph on one-direction timing and an aver-

Overleaf

54 (*top left*) A car that achieved victory in both Europe and America. Jimmy Murphy's Duesenberg which won the French Grand Prix with a 3-litre Duesenberg engine and the 1922 Indianapolis race with a Miller engine.

55 (*bottom left*) The last all-European car to win at Indianapolis was the Tipo 8CTF Maserati of Wilbur Shaw. Entered as the 'Boyle Special', it won the race in both 1939 and 1940.

56 (*right*) Bob Gerard scored an unexpected but well deserved second place with his ERA in the 1948 British Grand Prix. At one time he owned three of these cars.

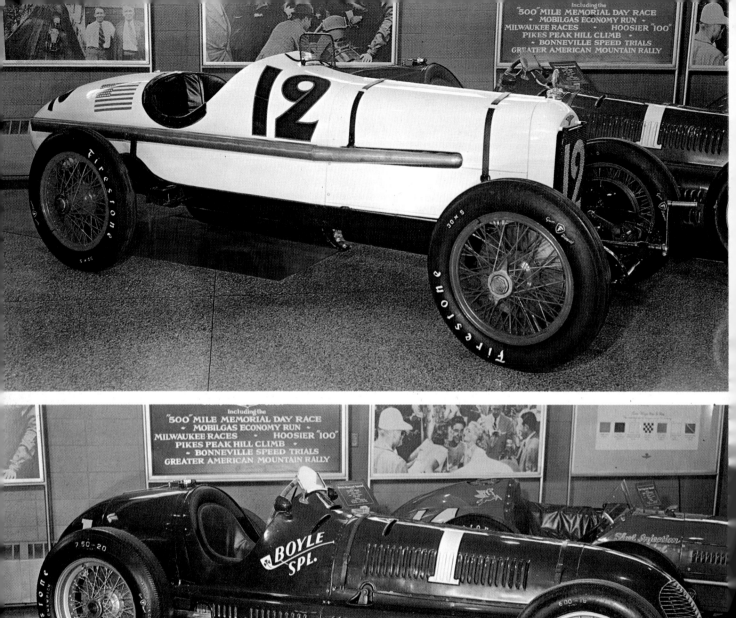
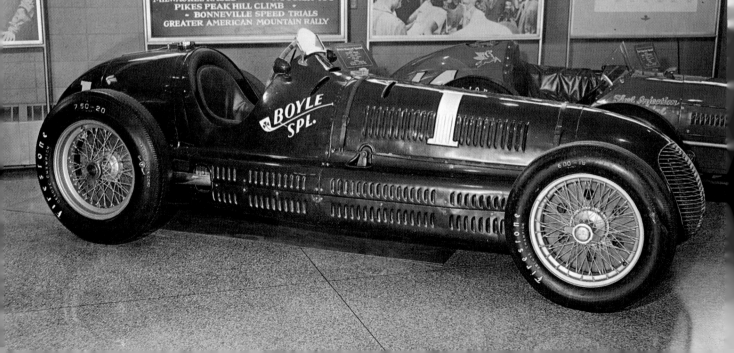

age of 164 mph over a flying mile at Muros Dry Lake in California. As the World Land Speed Record stood to Sir Malcolm Campbell at only 174 mph, Lockhart then decided to have a crack at this with a car fitted with two Miller 1,500 cc block assemblies on a common crankcase. At Daytona Lockhart was estimated to be travelling at 220 mph when a tyre burst and the driver was killed. The 1927 race went to the 1½-litre Duesenberg, but Millers occupied second and third places and won the event in both 1928 and 1929. Leon Duray with his front-wheel-drive '91' set a qualifying lap record for the 1928 race of 124·018 mph, and this record remained unbroken for nine years – the longest-standing record in the track's history.

In an effort to induce the mass-manufacturers to participate in racing and to give their large capacity, heavy, cast-iron engines an advantage, Indianapolis adopted a capacity limit of six litres from 1930 onwards, banned superchargers and added fuel capacity limits for 1934 and 1935. Not only did these regulations make life difficult for Miller, they also ruled out any hope of success for European cars. Nevertheless, the Maserati brothers fielded one of their *Sedici Cilindri* 4-litre cars there in 1930. With the removal of the superchargers went most of the car's performance and its driver, Baconin Borzacchini, achieved no success. These limitations did not deter Miller, whose designs continued to dominate Indianapolis. For 1931 Miller built a car with a de Dion rear end, thereby anticipating Mercedes' practice by some five years, and in addition produced a new 4-cylinder twin overhead camshaft engine of 2,988 cc. The new Miller engine was an immensely rigid unit and especial care in design was taken to facilitate stripping and assembly. There was a nickel cast-iron cylinder block with integral head, an aluminium alloy crankcase, four valves per cylinder and plain bearings. The immediate impact of the new design was slight, but with development it proved to have an excellent power output and a very fine torque range. Except for the Maserati victories in 1939 and 1940 and the victory of the 6-cylinder Thorne-Sparkes in 1946 (the only 6-cylinder car to have won the race apart from the Marmon Wasp), this Miller engine and derivatives of it, known as the Meyer-Drake and latterly as the Offen-

hauser, powered every Indianapolis winner from 1933 to 1964.

The Maserati [figure 55] which Wilbur Shaw drove to its two victories was the Tipo 8CTF 3-litre supercharged model which had such a dismal career in European racing. The supercharged Maserati became eligible for the race by the reversion in 1938 to the current European Formula; the capacity limits then adopted of 4,500 cc unsupercharged and 3,000 cc supercharged persisted until 1957, when the limit for unblown cars was reduced to 4,200 cc. Indianapolis racing cars of the late thirties and post-war years had, however, become so specialised for their particular type of racing that it was the general pattern for European cars to perform badly there, although they may have been exceedingly successful on their home ground. Among European cars to run at Indianapolis without acquitting themselves favourably have been, in 1946, works-prepared 8CL Maseratis, and, in 1952 and 1953, 4½-litre Ferraris, together with an outdated 8C-308 Alfa Romeo and a 1939 V-12 3-litre Mercedes-Benz. The Mercedes had been discovered in Czechoslovakia and its appearances at Indianapolis in 1947 and 1948 revealed that it was impossible to make such a complex car raceworthy once more without the works 'know-how'.

Among the more interesting cars to run at Indianapolis in post-war years have been the 'Blue Crown Spark Plug Specials'

Overleaf
58 The Alfa Romeo 158 in the wet at Silverstone with Juan Fangio at the wheel.

59 The technically very advanced front-wheel-drive 'Blue Crown Spark Plug Special' with Mauri Rose won the race in 1947 and 1948.

60 The huge 'Cummins Diesel Special' in which Freddie Agabashion set a new qualifying record of 138·010 mph for the 1952 race.

[figure 59], which won the race three years in succession, from 1947 to 1949. These were powered by the 4½-litre version of the Meyer-Drake engine, developing in this unsupercharged form some 300 bhp. The most notable feature of these cars, however, was front-wheel-drive, with the drive taken forward to the gearbox mounted at the front of the chassis frame and then to the front wheels by universally-jointed drive shafts. The front-wheel-drive theme has been carried on, alas unsuccessfully, by the 'Novi Specials', probably the most powerful cars ever to run at Indianapolis. These were powered by a 90-degree v8 engine of 2,762 cc (80 × 66·7 mm) with a supercharger compressing at 28 lb psi, which by 1966 had a power output of close to 700 bhp. This vast power was the weakness of the design and fantastically heavy front tyre wear ruined the chances of success even when engine trouble did not intervene.

To suit the peculiar conditions of racing at Indianapolis, a specialised breed of car emerged, with a tubular chassis by one of several component manufacturers, rigid axles front and rear, torsion bar suspension and a 2-speed gearbox with drive by torque-tube to a rear axle without differential. The 4½-litre Meyer-Drake engine, usually with Hilborn-Travers fuel injection, became the universal choice, the driver was seated very low to the right of the car and the engine was offset. There was little to differentiate the cars but the colour finishes and the names of their sponsors, and this traditional concept of the Indianapolis car, well loved by spectators, but static in development, persisted until 1964 and the last Offenhauser front-engined winner, the 'Sheraton Thompson Special' of A. J. Foyt. The first European rear-engined car, the Cooper of Jack Brabham, had taken seventh place at Indianapolis in 1961, and in 1963 the Lotus-Ford of Jim Clark was second. Clark's victory in the 1965 event completed the demise of the traditional 'Indy roadster'.

61 The 'Fuel Injection Special' which Bill Vukovich drove to victory in the 1953 and 1954 races.

62 The 'Bardahl Special' took third place in both the 1952 and 1953 races.

63 Last of the conventional Indianapolis winners was this Offenhauser-powered car with which A. J. Foyt won the 1964 race.

Overleaf
64 (*left*) The lorry-like reliability of the Lago-Talbot was well matched by 'Phiphi' Etancelin's driving methods. This French driver and car scored many successes in the early fifties.

65 (*right*) The Alfa Romeo 158 was one of the most successful racing cars of all time. Here a team of three of the Milanese cars are at Silverstone.

CHAPTER FIVE

An Era of Italian Domination 1946-51

IT is not possible to discuss Grand Prix racing of the immediate post-war years without looking back to its origins in the voiturette racing of ten years earlier. The overwhelming success of the German teams in Grand Prix racing had induced other racing car manufacturers to look for easier fields to conquer. From 1936 onwards Ettore Bugatti became increasingly and very successfully involved in sports car racing; the same year saw the appearance of the Maserati 6CM voiturette [figure 69], which had a number of features in common with the unsuccessful Maserati Grand Prix cars of the two preceding years. The twin overhead camshaft 6-cylinder 1,493 cc (65 × 75 mm) engine developed 155 bhp in its original form. This engine was based on that of the Type 34 Grand Prix car and in appearance the 6CM resembled the V-8RI. These new cars were tremendously successful in minor continental events, but were no real match for either Dick Seaman's rebuilt Delage of 1926-7 or the British ERAs. 6CMs, however, continued to be raced in post-war events and a very small number have survived.

The ERA [figures 70, 71] which first appeared in 1934, had been evolved from the 6-cylinder production Riley and its design followed much the same lines as the traditional Grand Prix cars of 1932-3. It was fast, rough and had very harsh semi-elliptic suspension. The 1,488 cc (57·5 × 95·2 mm) engine, with two high camshafts and short push-rods, a three-bearing crankshaft and Roots-type supercharger, developed 150 bhp in its original form. Transmission was by a Wilson pre-selector gearbox. By 1936 a total of seventeen of these cars had been

67 1951 World Champion Juan Fangio with John Cooper, builder of the Cooper-Bristol Formula 2 car.

66 (*opposite*) Duel of the Giants – the Alfa Romeos of Fangio and Farina lead the Ferraris of Ascari and Gonzalez in the 1951 Italian Grand Prix.

built and examples were raced with 1·1- and 2-litre engines as well as the original 1·5. The need for increased power output resulted in the appearance of the C-type cars with a Zoller vane-type supercharger, but all three cars were rebuilt versions of the earlier models. To cope with the increased power these cars also had Porsche independent front suspension by torsion bars, Lockheed hydraulic instead of Girling mechanical brakes and a ZF limited slip differential. These cars were highly successful in events of all types and the C type cars were virtually unopposed until the appearance of the 4CL Maserati in 1939. ERAs continued to be raced with success in post-war events and Bob Gerard was third in the 1948 RAC Grand Prix at Silverstone and second in the 1949 British Grand Prix. With the exception of one car, broken up after a fatal accident to its driver, all the early ERAs have survived and they are regular and consistent performers in Historic Racing Car events.

From these cars was developed the E-type ERA, of which two examples were built. The first appeared in 1939 and its chassis design was clearly inspired by the German Grand Prix cars. Front suspension was, as on the Auto Union, by the Porsche system, and the de Dion rear axle layout, which incorporated a synchromesh gearbox, was almost identical to that of the W154 Mercedes-Benz. The 1,487 cc (63 × 80 mm) engine was largely similar to that of the earlier ERAs and, fitted with a Zoller supercharger, developed 270 bhp at 7,500 rpm. In a long and protracted career, the E-type failed to win a single race. Eventually, in 1951, the engine of one of the cars which had been gutted in a fire was installed in the ex-Seaman Delage and the other E-type was rebuilt in 1955 as a Jaguar-powered sports car.

In 1938 the Alfa Romeo 158 [figures 58, 65, 66, 72, 81, 82, 83,

70 A successful British voiturette – this one is being driven by Raymond Mays, co-founder of the ERA organisation, in the 1938 BRDC Road Race at Brooklands. He finished second.

71 The Riley-based ERA engine was a 4-cylinder unit with twin high-mounted camshafts.

84, 85 & 87] had appeared as a rival to the Maserati 6CM and the 4CM which was the 6-cylinder chassis fitted with a 1,496 cc (69 × 100 mm) engine. In order that Italian cars should achieve a measure of success, in 1939 all Grand Prix on Italian soil were restricted to cars of 1,500 cc. It came as a shock, therefore, when Mercedes-Benz fielded two 1½-litre cars in the Tripoli Grand Prix. These, designated the W165, were virtually scaled-down versions of the W154 3-litre cars of 1938. The 8-cylinder in-line 64 × 58 mm engines, with the cylinders cast in two blocks of four, developed 260 bhp at 8,500 rpm. The chassis was almost identical to the Grand Prix cars and featured a de Dion rear axle layout, a 5-speed gearbox and offset engine and transmission. The Mercedes easily took first and second places, but they were never raced again.

At this time the Auto Union factory was at work on a V-2 1½-litre engine, but the outbreak of war prevented this from advancing beyond the early development stage. There was in fact every indication that the next Grand Prix Formula would restrict the capacity of supercharged engines to 1,500 cc, but the war delayed this change until 1946. At the same time the new Formula accommodated 4½-litre unsupercharged cars, as these, outclassed in pre-war Grand Prix racing, were thought to be fast enough to compete with the 1½-litre cars. For political

reasons, Germany was not admitted into Grand Prix racing, and
in any case neither Auto Union nor Mercedes-Benz were in a
position to build cars. Racing was, however, supported by both
Maserati and Alfa Romeo and their cars, which were both basically pre-war designs, are worthy of close study.

Alfa Romeo continued to race the 158 which had first
appeared in 1938 and was the design of Gioacchino Colombo.
The engine was a 1,479 cc (58 × 70 mm) design based on one
bank of cylinders of the 1938 3-litre v-16. The aluminium
cylinder block was cast in two 4-cylinder units with a
magnesium alloy crankcase and steel cylinder liners. In its original form, with a plain bearing crankshaft and a single-stage
supercharger, 190 bhp was developed at 6,500 rpm. Transmission was by a multi-plate dry-type clutch and a 4-speed
'crash' gearbox in unit with the final drive. The chassis was constructed from flat tubing, with the engine and final drive housing
acting as additional cross-members. The front suspension was
by trailing links and a six-leaf transverse leaf spring, while a
similar leaf spring and swing axles were used at the rear.

During 1938 the 158s won two races, but they were soundly
trounced by the new Mercedes at Tripoli in 1939, and out of
seven Alfas entered, only one finished, in third place. The result
of this defeat was that Alfa Romeo carried out extensive

75

74 The San Remo Maserati.

modifications to the design, including the fitting of a roller bearing crankshaft. Power output rose to 225 bhp at 7,500 rpm and the bodywork was restyled. Before Italy entered the war in 1940 the 158s gained four further victories against opposition that was far from strong. During the war years the Alfas were concealed in a cheese factory and they re-appeared in 1946 in twin-stage supercharged form with a power output of 260 bhp at 7,500 rpm. On their first post-war appearance at St Cloud, the two 158s entered retired with transmission trouble. This was merely teething trouble after the cars' long hibernation and they soon demonstrated that they were both faster and more reliable than any of their rivals. During the years 1946-8 Alfa Romeo entered 158s in eleven races and won every one. In 1947 the power output of the 158s rose to 310 bhp and at the end of the next year Alfa Romeo temporarily withdrew from racing. The reasons for this were partly financial and partly because new and strong opposition was anticipated from Ferrari and BRM.

During these three years Alfa Romeo's main opposition had come from Maserati, who were also racing a basically pre-war car. This was the Tipo 4CL, which had also made its debut on behalf of the works at Tripoli in 1939 and which was a considerable improvement on previous Maserati designs. A 4-cylinder engine of 1,489 cc (78 × 78 mm) was used and this featured four valves per cylinder and had a power output of 220 bhp at 8,000 rpm. The 4-speed gearbox was in unit with the engine and the channel-section frame had independent front suspension by torsion bars and double wishbones, with a rigid rear axle and quarter-elliptic springs. Of the three cars entered at Tripoli, one was a special streamlined model with a claimed maximum speed of 170 mph, driven by Luigi Villoresi. None of these cars, however, completed a single lap of the race. A win was gained in the 1940 Targa Florio before Italy entered the war and the cars reappeared in 1946. Whereas the Alfas were raced only by the works and were entered in only a small number of events, 4CL Maseratis were freely sold to private owners and could be seen racing at most events during the season.

A number of changes were made to the design of the 4CL during the early post-war years. In 1947 certain cars were raced with twin-stage superchargers which increased power output to 260 bhp at 7,000 rpm and towards the end of the season a new tubular frame was adopted. The same year the Maserati brothers sold their interests in the Company to Omer Orsi and in 1948 a much revised version, known as the 4CLT/48 [figure 76], appeared. Orsi had decided not to make further modifications to the engine, but in other respects the car had been almost completely redesigned. Wishbone and torsion bar front suspension had been a traditional Maserati feature since 1936, but Orsi adopted a system of wishbones and coil springs inclined inwards at an angle of forty-five degrees. The suspension at the rear was still quarter-elliptic springs, but they were longer and splayed out to a greater extent. A further new tubular frame was adopted, constructed from 4-inch-tubing sloping upwards at the front and passing under the rear axle. A train of gears in front of the final drive raised the line of the transmission, a feature necessitated by the lower build of the new chassis, and the bodywork was lower.

75 Post-war version of the 4CL was the 4CLT, seen here driven in the 1948 Jersey Road Race by Luigi Villoresi. He was unplaced.

These cars were sold to private owners and also raced on behalf of the works by the Scuderia Ambrosiana. They first appeared in the 1948 San Remo Grand Prix and afterwards became popularly known as the 'San Remo' model. The 4CLT/48 was slower than either the 158 Alfa or the new Ferrari which appeared in 1948, but handled well and was very reliable. During the years 1948-9, a large number of successes were gained, including wins in the 1949 San Remo and British Grands Prix, but as no efforts were made to develop the engines, the cars became increasingly outclassed. By 1950 they had a power deficiency of 70 bhp compared with the single plug 4½ litre Ferrari and 90 bhp compared with the Alfa 158.

In 1949 an attempt to re-hash the 4CLT/48 was made by the private Scuderia Milan team. The engine was fitted with a twin-plug cylinder head designed by Mario Speluzzi and power output was increased to 306 bhp at 7,000 rpm. Two of these cars ran without success in the 1949 Italian Grand Prix. Further modifications increased power output to 320 bhp for 1950 and one of the cars was fitted with a de Dion rear axle and transverse leaf spring. After some unsuccessful appearances during

76 From the 4CLT was developed the 4CLT/48 model which achieved a considerable degree of success in early post-war events. One is seen here driven by the Siamese driver, Bira.

77 The 4½-litre Lago-Talbot possessed almost lorry-like reliability and an excellent fuel consumption, but it did not have a great turn of speed. The car shown is driven by that courageous Belgian driver, Johnny Claes, and was finished in the Belgian racing colour, yellow.

that season, the Maserati-Milans were withdrawn from racing.

French participation in Grand Prix racing during these years was quite strong in numbers, but lacking in effectiveness. Apart from the odd pre-war Delahayes and two-seater Talbots, Antony Lago produced an entirely revised single-seater version of the Talbot [figure 77] to swell the ranks of the French cars for the 1948 season. Although the engine capacity of the new car remained at 4,482 cc (93 × 110 mm), the inclined overhead valves were now operated by short push-rods from camshafts mounted high up on the cylinder block after the manner of the pre-war ERAs. The porting arrangement had now been reversed so that the three Solex carburetters fed inlet ports on the right-hand side. Power output was 240 bhp at 4,800 rpm. Transmission was by single-plate clutch and Wilson pre-selector gearbox. The prop-shaft was offset to permit a lower seating position. Lubrication was on the dry sump principle, with twin oil coolers mounted on each side of the scuttle and projecting into the air stream.

Throughout 1948 and 1949 Talbots scored many successes in minor events on the Continent and Louis Rosier won the 1949 Belgian Grand Prix by running through the race without a refuelling stop and thereby defeating the works Ferraris. It was probably this victory which gave Enzo Ferrari his first doubts as to the advisability of running $1\frac{1}{2}$-litre supercharged cars with their inherently greater mechanical unreliability and higher fuel consumption. The Lago-Talbots, as the cars were now known, running on a mixture of petrol, ethanol and benzole, were averaging approximately 9 mpg, while in 1951 the Alfas, using a proportion of their fuel of mainly alcohol content for internal cooling, averaged about $1\frac{1}{2}$ mpg. During 1949 Louis Chiron also won for Talbot the Grand Prix de France.

For 1950 Lago produced a modified version of the $4\frac{1}{2}$-litre car with a twin-plug cylinder head, Zenith horizontal carburetters, a raised compression ratio and a power output of 280 bhp at 5,000 rpm. Talbots were now outclassed by both Alfa Romeo and Ferrari, but continued to do well in minor events. Rosier won the 1950 Albi Grand Prix and took second place at Pescara after Fagioli's Alfa broke its front suspension. Before the start of the 1951 season the Talbot factory found itself in severe financial difficulties and no more works cars were entered. Talbots continued to be raced by private owners, but after the existing Formula was scrapped in 1952 the cars' Grand Prix days were over. Although it failed to gain many outright wins in major events, the Lago-Talbot was a less expensive car to buy and race than the majority of its rivals and its successes were spread over six years of consistent racing. In addition the Talbot enjoyed a successful career in sports form and won the 1950 Le Mans twenty-four-hour race. Several racing Talbots still survive, including a pre-war two-seater and a late Formula One car, both of which have appeared in British Historic Racing Car events.

A brave, but completely unsuccessful, attempt to build a

78 The purposeful front-end of the 1½-litre supercharged Ferrari.

79 One of the first of the Grand Prix Ferraris – the privately-owned car of Peter Whitehead seen in the 1949 Jersey Road Race, where it finished seventh.

Grand Prix car from scratch was made in France soon after the war. This was the CTA-Arsenal initiated by the *Centre d'Etudes Techniques de l'Automobile et du Cycle* in 1946 with former Delage designer Albert Lory in charge of the project. The engine which was a twin overhead camshaft ninety-degree V-8 of 1,482 cc (60 × 65·5 mm), had twin superchargers in series compressing at 24 lb psi and developed 266 bhp at 7,500 rpm in bench tests. A rather outdated chassis design of sheet steel box-section construction was adopted, and suspension was independent on all four wheels by a system of vertical slides and torsion bars. The car first appeared at the 1947 French Grand Prix at Lyons, but non-started because a half-shaft broke on the line. By the following year's race at Rheims a second car had been completed, but both were withdrawn after trouble in practice. Neither car was raced again and they were eventually acquired by Antony Lago who had vague, but never fulfilled, plans for making them raceworthy. One of these cars is now on display in the Clères Musée d'Automobiles, which is situated off the road between Rouen and Dieppe.

1948 saw the appearance of an entirely new Italian Grand Prix car, the work of one of the most experienced designers and sponsored by the most experienced racing manager of all time. Enzo Ferrari's successes as entrant of Alfa Romeos on behalf of the works have been mentioned in an earlier chapter; after Alfa Corse had taken over the racing of works cars, Ferrari collaborated with Giaocchino Colombo in the design of the 158 Alfa and subsequently built two Fiat-based sports cars designed by Alberto Massimino. After the war Colombo designed for Ferrari a new and very advanced sixty-degree V-12 engine which first appeared in sports cars and was used from 1948 onwards in the new Ferrari Grand Prix car [figure 79]. This V-12 engine, which was largely of light alloy construction, had a single chain driven overhead camshaft per bank of cylinders and a capacity of 1,498 cc (55 × 52·5 mm). As used in the Grand Prix car, with a single-stage supercharger, power output was 225 bhp at 7,500 rpm.

The clutch and 5-speed constant-mesh gearbox were in unit with the engine and, as power output was rather lower than

the designer had anticipated, every effort was made to build the chassis as light as possible. This was a simple ladder-type tubular structure with suspension at the front by wishbones of unequal length and a transverse leaf spring. At the rear there was a swing axle layout with a transverse leaf spring mounted below and to the rear of the half-shafts and supplemented by a single radius arm on each side; a system of torsion bars was used at the rear on the early cars, but this was soon discarded.

The new Ferraris made their debut in the 1948 Italian Grand Prix at Turin, but of three entries, only Sommer finished, in third place. Retirements in both the Monza and Penya Rhin Grands Prix led to extensive development work during the winter months. The team acquired the services of Alberto Ascari and Luigi Villoresi, two leading Maserati drivers, and, with Alfa out of racing in 1949, a very successful season was expected. After a bad start in the Belgian Grand Prix at Spa, where the works cars were defeated by Rosier's Talbot, wins were gained in the Zandvoort Grand Prix, the *Daily Express* Trophy at Silverstone, the European Grand Prix at Monza and by Peter Whitehead with his private car in the Masaryk Grand Prix. The cars raced by the works at Monza were much improved; there were now twin overhead camshafts per bank of cylinders with gear instead of chain drive, and a twin-stage supercharger was fitted. These modifications increased power output to 300 bhp at 7,500 rpm. As well as having lower and smoother body lines, the

80 Luigi Villoresi with a 1½-litre supercharged car at the 1949 *Daily Express* Trophy at Silverstone.

new cars had an increased wheelbase and track.

1950 saw the return of the Alfa Romeo team to Grand Prix racing and provided exceptionally exciting racing. The power output of the 1958 Alfa was now 350 bhp at 8,500 rpm and the team of drivers – Farina, Fangio and Fagioli – was one of the most powerful ever seen in racing. Once again, the Alfa team was undefeated throughout the season, but the Ferraris were beginning to provide stiff opposition. At the end of 1949. Aurelio Lampredi replaced Colombo as Ferrari's chief designer and was given the task of redeveloping the basic V-12 engine to provide a 4½-litre unsupercharged unit for Grand Prix racing. While this was being prepared, however, Ferrari had to continue racing the existing and far from satisfactory 1½-litre cars.

The first clash between the two Italian teams came in the San Remo Grand Prix, where a solitary Alfa entered for Fangio easily defeated the two works four-cam Ferraris. The first three places were also taken by Alfa Romeo in the British Grand Prix, an event not entered by Ferrari. A week later both Alfa Romeo and Ferrari ran in the Monaco Grand Prix, but there was a multi-car crash on the first lap started by Farina spinning on a patch of water. Fangio, who was leading Farina, was not involved, and after working his way through the mêlée on his second lap went on to an easy victory from Ascari's four-cam Ferrari. The Swiss Grand Prix at Berne and the Belgian Grand Prix at Spa both saw the appearance of new Ferrari models, but to no avail – Alfa Romeo continued to dominate racing, with wins by Farina and Fangio respectively. At Berne, Villoresi drove a new short chassis supercharged car with a de Dion rear axle and a 4-speed gearbox, but this was eliminated by the failure of the de Dion tube, and also Ascari retired. Ascari drove the first of the new unsupercharged cars into fifth place at Spa, but it was not as yet sufficiently developed to provide the Alfas with any serious opposition. The new engine was a 3,322 cc (72 × × 68 mm) design with a single overhead camshaft per bank of cylinders and developing a modest 260 bhp. This was installed in one of the swing-axle long wheelbase chassis.

After the Dutch Grand Prix, in which the blown Ferraris were again defeated by the economical Talbot of Rosier which ran

81 The straight-eight engine of the 158 had a particularly neat and uncluttered appearance.

82 Note the left-hand gearchange, the rev. counter running up to 9000 rpm on this 1950 car (it ran to 10,000 on the 1951 159) and the *quadrifoglio*, the traditional Alfa 'four-leafed clover' badge, on the side of the scuttle.

83 The enormous brake drums of the 158 filled almost the full width of the wheel. Note the heavy ribbing for heat dissipation, and the air intake.

84 The 158 Alfa rear suspension, formed by swing axles and a transverse leaf spring.

through the race without a pit stop, Ferrari ran only unsupercharged cars in his attempt to defeat the Alfas; but it was not until the end of the season that they won a race. In the Grand Prix des Nations at Geneva, Villoresi drove the 3·3-litre car, while Ascari now had a car with a 4,080 cc (80 × 68 mm) engine developing 310 bhp and both cars had the de Dion rear axle. At the start Ascari led the entire Alfa team until Fangio was able to force his way past. Only seven laps from the end Villoresi crashed badly when in fifth position and Ascari was eliminated shortly afterwards by engine failure. The Italian Grand Prix at Monza saw the appearance of Ferraris with engines of a full 4,498 cc (80 × 74·5 mm) and developing 330 bhp [figure 88], but Alfa Romeo had managed to squeeze another 20 bhp out of the ageing twelve-year-old 158 and certain of the cars entered at Monza had improved brakes – these modified cars were known as the 159. Ascari actually led the race for two laps, but blew up his engine and took over Serafini's Ferrari to finish second. Farina with his Alfa won the race and thereby clinched the first ever Drivers' World Championship. The 4·5-litre Ferrari gained its first win at the end of the season in the Penya Rhin Grand Prix at Barcelona which Alfa Romeo did not enter.

In their endeavours to stave off the Ferrari challenge, the Alfa engineers were unwittingly making the 158 less reliable, and it became necessary to change such major components as crankshafts after only a few races. Nevertheless Satta (the chief designer) and Colombo, who had now returned to Alfa Romeo, extracted even more power out of the 158 for 1951. In bench tests it attained 10,500 rpm, could hold up to 9,500 rpm during a race with safety and was developing close to 400 bhp at 9,000 rpm – but at the expense of 135 bhp absorbed in driving the supercharger and a fuel consumption (using fuel containing 98 per cent methanol) of 1½ mpg. Four new cars were built for the 1951 season and although they had the usual 60-gallon fuel capacity, they appeared in some races with supplementary tanks installed in the cockpit and beside the engine. During 1951 the cars were also sometimes raced with de Dion rear axles.

The first clash between the two Italian teams came in the Swiss Grand Prix where Ferrari entered two new cars with twin plug cylinder heads increasing the power output to 380 bhp.

85 The veteran Fagioli was a driver of vast experience who had been in the pre-war Mercedes-Benz team. He is seen here in the 1950 British Grand Prix in which he took second place.

86 Alberto Ascari and Ferrari team-mate, Luigi Villoresi.

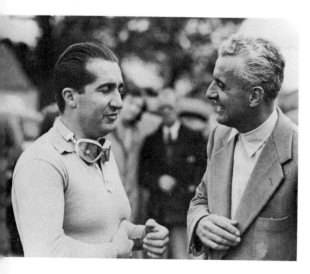

Although the race was won by Fangio's Alfa, Taruffi drove a very spirited race in his Ferrari and snatched second place from Farina a lap before the finish. The Belgian Grand Prix, held as always on the very fast Spa-Francorchamps circuit, was expected to favour the superior top end performance of the Alfas. Although the Ferraris were able to keep up with the Milanese cars in the early stages, as the Alfas were carrying vast quantities of fuel to eliminate the need for pit stops, Farina and Fangio soon began to gain ground. Then a fifteen-minute pit stop for Fangio left at the finish only one Alfa in front of the Ferraris of Ascari and Villoresi. The unsupercharged Ferraris already had better roadholding than their rivals and were now almost their equals in speed, whereas the Alfas were losing their reliability as the result of desperate efforts to increase power output. Ferrari came a step nearer his goal in the European Grand Prix at Rheims, for although Fangio's Alfa won the race, Ascari (who had taken over Gonzalez's Ferrari), Villoresi and Parnell (with the car privately owned by G. A. Vandervell and known as the 'Thin Wall Special') all finished ahead of Farina.

In the British Grand Prix at Silverstone, Froilan Gonzalez, in only his second race for Ferrari, provided the biggest shock of the 1951 season. At the wheel of one of the older single-plug cars he lapped in practice at 100·65 mph, over a second faster

than the quickest Alfa Romeo, and this was the first time that a car had lapped Silverstone at over 100 mph. In the race he brought the Ferrari to the chequered flag almost a minute ahead of Fangio's Alfa – the Alfa team's first defeat in six seasons of racing. This defeat was rubbed in and repeated in the German Grand Prix at the Nürburgring, a circuit well suited to Ferrari engine characteristics, for only Fangio of the Alfa team finished, beaten by Ascari and followed to the finish by Gonzalez, Villoresi and Taruffi. Alfa Romeo still felt that their cars had the upper hand on the very fast circuits and they were confident of a win in the Italian Grand Prix at Monza, where they entered four modified cars known as the 159M (the M denoted *Maggiorata* or improved). Alas, three of the Alfas retired and Farina, delayed by a leaking fuel tank, fought a lone and hopeless battle against the Ferraris of Ascari and Gonzalez, which took the first two places. The Alfa Romeo team did, however, have the consolation of a win in the season's last Grande Epreuve, the Spanish race, where the Ferraris were plagued by tyre trouble.

Unable to make their rear-engined flat 12 Tipo 512 model, which had been tested as early as 1942, into a raceworthy proposition, and unable to afford the cost of developing a new model, Alfa Romeo withdrew from racing. As Ferrari then

87 (*left*) The Alfa Romeo 158 team was one of the greatest and most memorable of racing organisations, particularly during 1950, when the principal drivers were the three 'F's, Italians Dr Giuseppe Farina and Luigi Fagioli and the Argentinian Juan Manuel Fangio. The picture shows Farina in the 1951 British Grand Prix at Silverstone, in which he retired with clutch trouble.

88 (*right*) Gonzalez presses on to victory in the 1951 British Grand Prix.

89 The most highly developed 4½-litre Ferrari was the 'Thin Wall Special' owned by Tony Vandervell. It is seen here in its most developed form with disc brakes, a new body, twin-plug cylinder head and revised exhaust system. Mike Hawthorn is at the wheel.

appeared to be completely unchallenged in the field of Grand Prix racing and the new 2½-litre Grand Prix Formula was not due to come into operation until 1954, the race organisers switched to Formula Two regulations. Thus the effective racing career of the 4½-litre Ferrari, apart from minor events and cars built for Indianapolis, was brought to an untimely end.

There was, however, one car which should have provided an effective challenge to Ferrari and have injected sufficient life into the existing Grand Prix Formula to make it last a further two years. This was the BRM. V-16 [figure 68] which had first appeared in 1949. The BRM was the brainchild of Raymond Mays and Peter Berthon, who received financial and other aid from a large number of British industrial concerns and private individuals. It is clear, in retrospect, that the BRM was over-complex and possessed a number of serious design faults. The engine was a V-16 of 1,496 cc (49·53 × 47·8 mm) with twin overhead camshafts driven by a spur gear train from the centre of the crankshaft and a twin-stage centrifugal supercharger. In its final form, the BRM developed a reliable 525 bhp at 10,500 rpm. A 5-speed all-indirect gearbox was fitted and suspension at the front was by Porsche-type trailing arms and Lockheed air struts, while at the rear there was a de Dion axle and the air struts were again used.

Throughout their career, which began with half-shaft failure at the start of the 1950 *Daily Express* Trophy at Silverstone and ceased with the cars running in minor *Formule Libre* events in 1955, they were plagued by mechanical trouble. Even in their last season they could not be relied upon to finish in a 10-lap race. It became evident at an early stage in the career of the BRM that the centrifugal type of supercharger was basically unsuitable for use in a racing car, and engine, suspension and braking troubles took far longer to cure than was reasonable. In many ways the V-16 BRM was a tragic and shameful wast of money, but it was also a magnificent folly. The sound of those sixteen cylinders in full song has rarely been matched and the occasional demonstration appearances of the cars are still exciting to watch.

Survivors of this magnificent era of racing are few, apart from the ERAs, BRMs and Talbots, for it was Ferrari's practice to break up his racing cars once their working life was over and the only Alfas were the works cars. Although they are not on exhibition, it is believed that two 159s survive at the Alfa factory. The late Tony Vandervell's 'Thin Wall Special' Ferrari is also still carefully preserved. This was raced in British events until the end of the 1954 season, by which time it had been developed into the most potent of all 4½ litre Ferraris.

90 The very elaborate Osca V-12 engine which was mounted in a Maserati 4CLT/48 chassis and raced by the Siamese driver Prince Bira. Note Bira's 'White Mouse Stable' badge on the scuttle.

CHAPTER SIX

A Substitute Formula 1952-3

91 Mike Hawthorn at Silverstone in 1953 with his Formula Two Ferrari.

92 (*opposite*) The last successful Ferrari Formula Two car was the Tipo 500 4-cylinder model seen here driven at Silverstone in 1953 by Mike Hawthorn.

ALTHOUGH Formula Two did not achieve World Championship status until 1952, following the withdrawal from racing of Alfa Romeo, the category, which limited the capacity of unsupercharged cars to 2,000 cc and supercharged cars to 500 cc, had been introduced by the Fédération Internationale de l'Automobile for the 1948 season. It was in every way a less expensive Formula than Formula One and competitive cars could be built for about £2,500 ($6,000), although it must be admitted that the Ferraris which dominated the Formula cost a great deal more to develop and build.

The first Ferrari to appear in Formula Two racing was the Tipo 166 Corsa. In general design the engine was similar to that of the early Ferrari Grand Prix car described in the preceding chapter, but it was, of course, unsupercharged and its capacity had been increased to 1,995 cc (60 × 58.8 mm). In this form 130 bhp was developed at 7,000 rpm and two-seater bodywork was fitted. During 1948 the Corsa won three races and in the following year Ferrari raced the Grand Prix chassis powered by a 2-litre engine. Although these cars had more than adequate power to deal with the opposition, they did not handle too well and towards the end of the year Ferrari produced a revised version with a chassis nine inches longer – 7 ft 10 in. For 1950 the Formula Two cars were drastically revised; the swing-axle rear suspension was replaced by a de Dion axle located by twin radius arms, a lower and lighter frame with a 7 ft 6 in wheelbase and a 4-speed gearbox in unit with the final drive. Power output had now risen to 158 bhp at 7,000 rpm. During 1950 and

93 An early V-12 Formula Two Ferrari seen here driven by Bill Dobson at Goodwood in 1952.

1951 these cars scored a large number of successes, although, like their Formula One counterparts, they suffered a great deal from transmission trouble.

By the spring of 1951, however, Aurelio Lampredi had a completely new 4-cylinder Ferrari Formula Two car [figure 92], ready to race, which possessed much improved low speed torque and was capable of lapping the slower circuits faster. This was the Tipo 500 with a capacity of 1,980 cc (90 × 78 mm) and with twin overhead camshafts driven by a train of gears from the nose of the crankshaft. Power output was approximately 160 bhp at 7,000 rpm. The 4-speed gearbox was in unit with the final drive which incorporated a ZF limited slip differential. The tubular ladder-type chassis had front suspension by wishbones of unequal length and at the rear there was a de Dion axle with twin radius arms and a transverse leaf spring. The Tipo 500 made successful appearances at Modena during 1951 and it was with this model that Ferrari entered Grand Prix events during 1952 and 1953.

Ferrari's chief opposition during these two years of racing came from the Maserati concern, who produced a new model for the 1952 season. Since the acquisition of the Modena concern by Omer Orsi, there had been a distinct reluctance to produce new models. In 1947 the Maserati brothers had built the 6-cylinder single overhead camshaft 1,488 cc (66 × 72.5 mm) A6 sports car with an engine design following very closely that of the 1936 6CM voiturette, but the newer car was unsupercharged and developed a very modest 65 bhp. Later the same year appeared a development of the A6, the A6GCS which had a twin overhead camshaft 2-litre engine and a power output of 125 bhp at 5,500 rpm. The A6GCS appeared in a number of Formula Two events during 1948, but no attempts were made to develop the design further. In 1951, however, a design team led by Alberto Massimino used the A6GCS as a basis for a new Formula Two car raced during the 1952 season. The new car, the Tipo A6GCM [figure 95], had a 6-cylinder engine with a capacity of 1,988 cc (75 × 75 mm) and with twin overhead camshafts driven by a train of gears from the front of the crankshaft. With three twin-choke Weber

carburetters, power output was 165 bhp. Both in appearance and chassis design the new car had much in common with the 4CLT/48, including the retention of a live rear axle suspended on quarter-elliptic springs.

After an inauspicious debut in the Argentine races at the beginning of the year, the Maseratis met the works Ferraris in the non-Championship Autodrome Grand Prix at Monza in June. Maserati had been fortunate in securing the services of Fangio, Gonzalez and Felice Bonetto, but although the cars showed a considerable turn of speed, Fangio was eliminated by a crash which put him out of racing for the rest of the season and the other two cars suffered mechanical troubles. The works Maseratis did not again put in an appearance until the German Grand Prix in August, where a solitary car, entered for Bonetto, retired. Two cars with much improved gearboxes and 12-plug cylinder heads, which increased the power output to 177 bhp, were entered in the Italian Grand Prix in September for Gonzalez and Bonetto. For the first time in a season in which Ferraris had already won six Grandes Epreuves and eleven other races, they were faced with serious opposition. Gonzalez took the lead at the fall of the flag and led until forced to make a pit stop for fuel and tyres. As a result Ascari was again the winner, but Gonzalez took a very worthy second place.

For 1953 only minor modifications were made to the Ferraris, but the Maseratis were largely redesigned by Giaocchino

94 (*left*) The later and lower V-12 Ferrari with de Dion rear axle which Ascari drove into third place in the 1950 Dutch Grand Prix.

95 (*right*) In 1952 Maserati entered Formula Two racing with the 6-cylinder A6GCM. Froilan Gonzalez took second place in the 1952 Italian Grand Prix with this dual ignition car.

Overleaf
96 (*left*) The Connaught was another successful British design built with limited financial backing. Some of these cars still appear in Historic Racing Car events and this example is seen at Castle Combe in 1965.
97 (*right*) Light and with excellent handling characteristics, but underpowered because it had only a tuned touring car engine, the Cooper-Bristol performed well in the hands of Mike Hawthorn and other British drivers. Here, Ken Wharton, one of the most versatile drivers of all time, is seen at the wheel of the car he drove in 1953.

98 Directly developed from the 1952 car was the following year's A6SSG. This is Felice Bonetto in the 1953 British Grand Prix.

99 The 6-cylinder Osca was very fast, but was never driven sufficiently well to really show its paces.

Colombo, who had now joined the Modena concern. The engine dimensions were revised to 76·2 × 72 mm and power output rose to 190 bhp at 8,000 rpm, the frame was strengthened and a lower and far more attractive body was fitted. Throughout the 1953 season the Maseratis, now designated the A6SSG, were improved in both speed and reliability, although their roadholding never matched that of the Ferraris. After third places at Zandvoort and Spa, Maserati came close to victory at Rheims, where Hawthorn's Ferrari defeated Fangio's Maserati by only a second. An exciting and closely fought season reached its climax in the Italian Grand Prix at Monza, where Maserati finally gained a victory. After a very close race, Ascari spun the leading Ferrari at the last corner, enabling Fangio to gain a narrow victory from Farina's Ferrari.

The Italian Grand Prix also saw the introduction of a new Ferrari which was a prototype for the 1954 season. This was the Tipo 553, which had a multi-tubular 'space frame' (with suspension similar to that of the Tipo 500) and a 1,997 cc (93 × 73·5 mm) engine, and was distinguishable by wide, squat bodywork resulting from the use of side-mounted fuel tanks. The Monza race was purely a try-out for these cars and they were driven by the most junior members of the Ferrari team.

Although the years of the 2-litre Formula were largely dominated by the works Ferraris and Maseratis, there were a large number of other interesting contenders, including some from Italy. For 1952 Enrico Platé, a Swiss entrant of Maseratis since early post-war days, rebuilt his two 4CLT/48 cars to comply with Formula Two Regulations. The chassis were shortened by a little over eight inches, corresponding to the space formerly taken up by the superchargers, there were new cylinder blocks with a capacity of 1,995 cc (84 × 90 mm), and the cars could be distinguished by a shorter and more rounded radiator grille. Power output was 150 bhp at 7,000 rpm and, as the cars were on the heavy side, they were much slower than the Italian works cars. In 1953 Platé raced one of the latest A6SSG Maseratis.

Another Italian effort was the Osca Formula Two car [figure 99] built by the Maserati brothers in their small works at Bologna. With twin overhead camshafts driven from a train of gears from the nose of the crankshaft and three twin-choke Weber carburetters, the 6-cylinder 1,987 cc (76 × 73 mm) engine developed a healthy 160 bhp at 6,300 rpm. The chassis was a simple tubular ladder-type structure with double wishbone and coil spring front suspension and a de Dion rear axle. One of these comparatively simple but swift cars was driven during the 1952 season by Elie Bayol and this was joined in 1953 by a second car for Louis Chiron, the veteran Monagasque who had been a member of the Scuderia Ferrari team in pre-war days. Chiron's car performed particularly consistently and took second places at Syracuse and Aix-les-Bains.

At one time there was close cooperation between the Maserati brothers and the French constructor Amédée Gordini. In pre-war days Gordini had modified Simca-built Fiats for competition use and from 1946 onwards he raced single-seater cars based on the 1,098 cc Simca-Fiat overhead valve unit. These cars were known as Simcas and Gordini was financed by the Simca company. By 1948, 1,430 cc versions had appeared and with a Wade supercharger they used to perform in Formula One events. In 1951 Simca allowed Gordini to produce a 1,496 cc 4-cylinder twin overhead camshaft engine, as there was a possibility that they could use this in their more sporting production cars. The new Simca engine still gave away 500 cc to its rivals and Gordini was tired of Simca holding the purse-strings. From 1952 and with very limited financial resources Gordini raced under his own name cars powered by 6-cylinder 1,986 cc (75 × 75 mm) twin overhead camshaft engines developing 155 bhp at 6,000 rpm [figure 100]. As he was hampered by his financial difficulties and as the engine design was insufficiently developed, Gordini's entries were often ill-prepared and their flimsy construction resulted in frequent mechanical failures. Their successes were few, but Jean Behra's car succeeded in defeating the works Ferraris in the 1952 Rheims Grand Prix.

Among the staunchest supporters of Formula Two racing were the British constructors. The greatest of these was the HWM team of John Heath and his partner George Abecassis. During 1949 they raced the HW-Alta [figure 103] with a 1,960 cc (79 × 100 mm) twin overhead camshaft 4-cylinder Alta engine and

100 The French Gordini was also very fast – but fragile. Mechanical failures were frequent and the cars achieved success only in minor events.

Overleaf
101 (*left*) The 1957 version of the Maserati 250F with World Champion Juan Fangio at the wheel in practice for the 1957 British Grand Prix.
102 (*right*) The car that scored the first British victory in a major Grand Prix since Segrave's win with a Sunbeam at Tours in 1923. The race was the 1957 British Grand Prix and the car was the Vanwall. Here it is driven by Tony Brooks, but Stirling Moss took over later in the race.

103 The original HW-Alta of 1949 had a 125 bhp engine and two-seater bodywork which permitted it to run in sports car events.

104 By 1952 the HWM was a refined but still essentially practical design. It still lacked, however, sufficient power to match the Ferraris.

two-seater bodywork. Encouraged by the performance of this car, Heath built a team of three cars [figure 104], now known simply as HWMs, for the 1950 season. These retained the tubular chassis and wishbone and transverse leaf spring independent front suspension of the 1949 car, but there was also a similar system of suspension at the rear. The season's successes included a win in the Grand Prix des Frontières and the following year a total of five new cars were built, but with single-seater bodywork, coil spring front suspension and a de Dion rear axle. Among the team's drivers during these years were Stirling Moss, who gained his first experience of real racing cars with HWM, and Peter Collins, later a works Ferrari driver, who drove for the team in 1952 and 1953. Although the power output of the HWM rose to 130 bhp at 6,000 rpm in 1952 and to 160 bhp in 1953, the cars were still too underpowered to be competitive and, in addition, were rather heavy. Few successes were gained during 1953 and a works car fitted for the 1954 season with a 2,464 cc (86 × 106 mm) Alta engine was completely outclassed in Grand Prix racing. Several of the works cars were rebuilt as Jaguar-engined sports cars after being disposed of by the works, but among survivors of the make are a 1950 two-seater, largely in its original condition, and a single-seater car fitted with a Jaguar engine.

The Alta engine was the work of Geoffrey Taylor, who had been building racing cars and engines since 1930. In 1948 Taylor had produced a Grand Prix car with a 1,490 cc (78 × 78 mm) 4-cylinder engine developing in its most advanced form ·230 bhp at 7,000 rpm. Three of these cars were supplied to private owners, but by 1950 Taylor had become more interested in Formula Two and the following year there appeared a car powered by the same engine as used in the later HWMs, a 1,960 cc (82·5 × 90 mm) unit developing in this form 150 bhp at 6,000 rpm. The chassis design of the Formula Two car was similar to that of the Grand Prix model and had a twin-tube chassis and independent suspension front and rear by double wishbones compressing on to rubber blocks. During their three seasons of racing the cars never showed any real form, and Coopers powered by Alta engines achieved little more success.

A 1951 2-litre Alta has survived and has appeared frequently in Historic Racing Car events.

The lack of a suitable high-performance power unit hampered British constructors whose chassis designs were generally in advance of Continental practice. The Connaught concern of Send in Surrey endeavoured to overcome this difficulty by using a derivative of the Lea-Francis push-rod engine, which had already powered Connaught sports cars. The first Formula Two car [figure 96] which apeared in 1950 had the normal Lea-Francis capacity of 1,760 cc, but the engine had been fitted with a special light alloy crankcase and had been tuned to develop 135 bhp. The chassis was a tubular ladder-type structure with wishbone and torsion bar front suspension and a similar system at the rear, but the latter was subsequently changed to a de Dior layout. After a great deal of development work and racing experience with the prototype, further cars were built for the 1952 season. They had an engine of 1,960 cc (79 × 100 mm), and with one of these Dennis Poore took an excellent fourth place

105 A 1952 Alta Formula Two car.

Overleaf
106 (*left*) The B-series Connaught in the form in which it won the 1955 Syracuse Grand Prix.

107 (*right*) The cockpit of the Syracuse Connaught. Note the gear-lever for the pre-selector box.

in the 1952 British Grand Prix. During the 1953 season the Connaught concern ran a full works team in major international races. Certain of the works cars were fitted with the American Hilborn-Travers fuel injection system and to boost power output the team also experimented with nitro-methane, a foul-smelling fuel of high potency and costing around £10 ($24) per gallon. In major events, the cars lacked sufficient power to race on even terms with Ferrari and Maserati, but their record in British National events was excellent. In all, nine of these cars were built and several are still raced.

The only other British power unit suitable for Formula Two use was the Bristol, a 6-cylinder 1,971 cc (66 × 96 mm) unit, identical in almost all respects to the pre-war BMW '328' sports car engine. This was a rather unusual push-rod overhead valve design featuring supplementary cross-over push-rods so as to avoid the necessity for using twin overhead camshafts. As well as powering the production Bristol saloons, this unit was used in the very specialist and very expensive Frazer Nash sports cars, but its maximum power output in 1952 form was a very modest 127 bhp at 5,800 rpm. The first Formula Two user of this engine was the Cooper Company, who built a very light car (their only front-engined racing car) with a chassis built up from drilled box-section side-members and a tubular superstructure and with wishbone and transverse leaf spring suspension

108 (*left*) The unconventional G-type ERA with offset driving position and the engine angled in the frame formed the basis of the Bristol 450 sports/racing cars.

109 (*right*) The 4-cylinder Connaught engine based on the Lea-Francis 14 hp unit.

front and rear. For 1953 a fully tubular chassis was adopted and power output was increased to 150 bhp [figure 97]. In all twenty of these cars were built, including examples with ERA and Alta engines. In their first season one of the earliest cars especially tuned by his father was driven by the young Mike Hawthorn and his skilful and exuberant driving, which gained him fourth places in both the European Grand Prix at Spa and the Dutch Grand Prix, made a tremendous impact on the racing scene. The Bristol engine was also used in the Frazer Nash and ERA G-type Formula Two cars, while developments of the original BMW engine powered both the German AFM and Veritas cars.

Historic Racing Car events are rich in survivors of this era of racing and both Cooper-Bristols and Connaughts can still be seen performing at Silverstone and elsewhere. All old racing cars are expensive and difficult to maintain, and spares are not easy to come by; but these problems are not so acute with the comparatively modern and simple Formula Two cars.

110 Stirling Moss, who entered Grand Prix racing at the wheel of John Heath's HWMs.

An Era of Unsupercharged Racing 1954-60

THE Grand Prix Formula of the years 1954-60 was the longest lived of all Formulae and stimulated designs of considerable technical diversity and racing of exceptional interest. The Formula was a direct follow-on from Formula Two and it was only logical that the first cars raced should be models designed for the earlier Formula with engine capacity increased to the new limit of 2,500 cc. The capacity limit for supercharged cars was increased to 750 cc, but experience had shown that engine development was insufficiently advanced to build a supercharged unit that could match the power output of the unblown cars. The provision for supercharged cars had been made only because BRM had expressed the intention of building an engine based on one half of their V-16 unit.

No completely new cars appeared during the first few months of the Formula, as the Italian teams were perhaps rather too complacent about the performances of their cars during the preceding two years, and Gordini could afford no new cars as his financial position was still acute. The Gordinis had their engines enlarged from 1,986 cc (75 × 75 mm) to 2,475 cc (84 × 80 mm), an engine size used in Gordini sports cars during 1953, but otherwise the design was completely unchanged and still retained a live rear axle. Gordini had always been preoccupied with building his cars as light as possible to counteract their power deficiency – a deficiency which could only be overcome by an intensive development programme which he could not afford – but, despite this, the enlarged engines were too fast for the chassis and mechanical failures were frequent. Out of

112 For the 1954 season a couple of the Formula Two HWMs were fitted with 2½-litre Alta engines. The works car, driven by Lance Macklin, had SU fuel injection and is seen here at Goodwood. The cars were very slow and soon disappeared from the racing scene.

111 (opposite) The power-packed bonnet of the 1960 Aston Martin DBR4/250.

45 Gordini entries which started in Grandes Epreuves (events counting towards the World Championship) during 1954 and 1955, only eleven finished, and during these two years the make scored only two victories: in the 1954 Bordeaux Grand Prix where Jean Behra won after the leading Ferrari broke its crankshaft, and at the rather parochial Circuit of Cadours which no other works teams entered.

Ferrari raced two models, the Tipo 625 'Argentina' [figure 113] and the Tipo 555 [figure 114], known familiarly, because of its shark-like appearance, as the 'Squalo'. The Argentina, a 2,490 cc version of the Formula Two Tipo 500, had been raced in the Bari Grand Prix in prototype form as long ago as 1951 and had appeared in 1953 at both the *Formule Libre* Buenos Aires Grand Prix and the Rouen Grand Prix run to the 'old' Formula One regulations. Power output of the 625 in its 1954 form was 230 bhp at 7,000 rpm compared with 200 bhp when it first appeared in 1951. The 'Squalo' was identical to the 553 which had appeared at Monza in 1953, but with an engine of 2,497·56 cc (100 × 79·5 mm) and developing 250 bhp at 7,500 rpm. Throughout the 1954 season the 625s were popular with drivers because of their good handling, but on most circuits lacked sufficient speed, while the 555s, despite having stronger engines with more rigid crankshaft webbing and enlarged bearing area, were mechanically unreliable and handled badly. As a result Ferrari carried out many engine experiments during the year with a view to gaining both increased reliability and power output.

113 (*left*) Froilan Gonzalez on his way to victory in the 1954 British Grand Prix with a Tipo 625 Ferrari.

114 (*right*) The 555, known familiarly as the 'Squalo' because of its shark-like appearance, was identical – apart from engine capacity – to the Ferrari Tipo 553 prototypes which had appeared at Monza in 1953.

The 1954 Maserati was known as the 250F [figures 101, 115 and 116] and was a version of the 1953 A6SSG extensively revised by Giaocchino Colombo. The bore of the 6-cylinder engine was increased from 76·6 mm to 84 mm, giving a capacity of 2,493 cc and power output rose from 200 to 240 bhp at 7,400 rpm. Colombo scrapped the archaic rigid axle layout and tubular frame of the A6SSG and replaced them with a new multi-tubular 'space-frame' having two widely spaced side-members with the lower tubes sweeping upwards at the front and the rear and a de Dion rear axle layout; the de Dion axle was attached to a transverse leaf spring and the tube passed in front of the gearbox. Unfortunately this axle layout did not prove completely reliable and was the cause of a number of retirements during the season. Subtle changes to the lines of the car had turned it into one of the best looking racing cars of its time and until the Maserati works withdrew from racing at the end of the 1957 season, it was the most consistently successful car. Whereas Ferrari, heavily financed by the Fiat organisation and racing for prestige purposes, normally sold only touring and sports models, Maserati put the 250F into limited production – in all thirty-two were built and a number of cars were ordered by private owners for racing in 1954. Among these purchasers were Stirling Moss, Gilby Engineering who bought a car for Roy Salvadori to drive, and the Owen Organisation who wanted a car to race until the new 2½-litre BRM was ready.

The first two major events of the 1954 season, the Argentine

115 (*left*) As well as being successfully raced by the works, Maserati 250Fs were sold to private owners at a price of around £5,000. The car shown was owned by Gilby Engineering and driven by Roy Salvadori.

116 (*right*) The twin overhead camshaft 6-cylinder engine of the Maserati 250F.

and Belgian Grands Prix, were won by the Maserati of Juan Manuel Fangio, but the French Grand Prix held at Rheims saw the debut of the new Mercedes-Benz W196 [figures 117 and 118] and a change in the old order of domination of Grand Prix racing by Italian cars. The discipline and efficiency of the Mercedes team in pre-war days had been so impressive that they re-entered racing with a reputation for being unbeatable and even the Italian teams, whose staff included a number of pre-war Scuderia Ferrari and Alfa Romeo personnel, expected a Mercedes victory. In addition Mercedes-Benz had the advantage of starting with a clean drawing board and no preconceived ideas as to design layout. The Mercedes engineers, led by Rudolph Uhlenhaut, chose an in-line 8-cylinder engine with a capacity of 2,496 cc (76 × 68·8 mm). This was claimed to develop 270 bhp . 8,200 rpm, which meant that it was rather more powerful than any of its rivals, and was mounted in the frame almost horizontally so as to give a very low bonnet, but it was necessary to remove the right-hand front wheel and a body panel before the sparking plugs could be changed. Most designers would have preferred a vee-engine layout because of the shorter overall length and the increased stiffness of the crankshaft. At this time, however, Grand Prix cars were still comparatively bulky and heavy and the overall length of the engine was relatively unimportant, especially as it was possible to achieve a smaller frontal area with an in-line engine. Two very advanced features of the engine design were the Bosch direct fuel injection instead of carburetters and desmodromic valves; the very high compression ratio of 17 : 1 was used partly because a high pressure was required, in the absence of valve springs, to ensure that the valves shut after being returned close to their seats by the return cam. The engine was built up of individual cylinders surrounded by a sheet metal cowling which formed a water jacket (a feature derived from pre-war Mercedes practice), the cylinder head was non-detachable, and the crankshaft was divided in two for rigidity with the drive taken off by a pair of gear wheels in the middle of the engine.

In choosing a rear suspension for the W196, the Mercedes designers rejected the de Dion layout which they had resurrec-

117 (above) Mercedes-Benz had the advantage of re-entering racing with no preconceived ideas and a highly skilled engineering team. Fangio won the 1954 Italian Grand Prix at Monza with this streamlined car, but only after the retirement of Stirling Moss' Maserati in the closing stages of the race.

118 (*below*) This view of the Mercedes-Benz entries at Silverstone reveals a number of very interesting features including the detachable steering wheel, the right-hand gearchange and the very neat panel-work of the tail section.

ted in 1937 for a swing axle system of a new type. With the conventional swing axle layout, the drive shafts are housed within the swinging axle halves, but the W196 had two transverse swinging links, locating the wheels laterally, and these were integral with the wheel hubs and met at a common pivot point at the centre-line beneath the rear-mounted gearbox housing. The wheels were mounted longitudinally by an upper leading and a lower trailing link per wheel so that a Watts linkage was formed on either side of the car. The suspension itself was formed by longitudinal torsion bars and finned telescopic hydraulic dampers. With this layout the transverse links were much longer than the swing axle halves, so that the variation of camber angle and, therefore, tyre scrub, was reduced considerably. At the front, the wheels were located by two pairs of wishbones and torsion bars were again used. The frame of the Mercedes, constructed from small diameter tubing, was clothed in a very unusual aerodynamic streamlined body, but it was clear that the engineers had not complete faith in this body, for although all the area within the very deep frame was put to good use, nothing was carried in the space between the front and rear wheels.

So successful were the new German cars that the 1954 and 1955 seasons were remarkable for the races which they did not win. At Rheims the Mercedes of Fangio and Kling took first and second places and Herrmann's car set the fastest lap. The entire Ferrari team retired with engine trouble in their vain pursuit of the Mercedes and only two Maseratis, out of eight entered, finished. The next race counting towards the World Championship, the British Grand Prix at Silverstone, showed the drawbacks of the streamlined bodywork and the deficiencies of Mercedes roadholding. Silverstone is a bleak and rather featureless medium speed circuit with, at that time, many of the corners marked by oil drums; it was, in addition, particularly well suited to Ferrari engine and suspension characteristics. Tipo 625 Argentinas driven by Froilan Gonzalez and Mike Hawthorn took first and second places. Fangio finished an unhappy fourth with the bodywork of the Mercedes battered by contact with oil drums, the brakes fading, the gears jumping out and an oil leak. At the European Grand Prix at the Nurbürgring, Mercedes introduced an unstreamlined model with conventional bodywork and won both this race and the Swiss Grand Prix. A further win by the streamlined car was gained at Monza in the Italian Grand Prix, but only after the retirement of the leading Maserati driven by Stirling Moss.

The final Grande Epreuve of the season, the Spanish Grand Prix held on the Pedralbes circuit through the streets of Barcelona, was a race of exceptional interest, for it saw the defeat of Mercedes at the hands of Hawthorn with an improved version of the 'Squalo' Ferrari with coil spring front suspension, the first Ferrari model to be so fitted, and the first race appearance of the long awaited Grand Prix Lancia D50 [figure 120]. The designer of the Lancia was Vittorio Jano whose previous work included the Alfa Romeo Monoposto and the Lancia sports/racing cars. Unlike the Mercedes, which had been built to achieve a certain performance almost regardless of the complications and the size and weight penalties involved, the Lancia was lighter, lower and shorter than other Grand Prix cars of the period and was of fairly simple design. Despite its many advanced features, the Mercedes was a 'blind alley' in development, for the trend was increasingly towards smaller and lighter cars and the Lancia was the trend-setter. To power his new design Jano chose a ninety-degree v-8 unit with a capacity of 2,487 cc (73·6 × 73·1 mm), twin chain-driven overhead camshafts per bank of cylinders, four twin-choke Solex carburetters, twin plugs per cylinder and a power output of 260 bhp at 8,000 rpm. Double wishbone suspension was used at the front and a de Dion axle and twin radius rods at the rear, in both cases with a transverse leaf spring. The frame was a multi-tubular structure and the engine, which was canted so that the driver could sit alongside the propshaft, formed an integral stiffener. The 5-speed gearbox, in unit with the final drive, had Porsche baulk-ring synchromesh on the upper four ratios. To keep the weight within the wheelbase and to prevent the handling being affected by changes in the fuel level, pannier fuel tanks were mounted on struts between the wheels.

At Barcelona, the Lancia of Ascari was fastest in practice, but

both cars entered retired early in the race, and all three entries were eliminated in the 1955 Argentine Grand Prix. After minor successes at Pau, Turin and Naples early in the 1955 season, Scuderia Lancia entered a team of four cars in the Monaco Grand Prix, a particularly slow and difficult race. The race was notable for the retirement of the Mercedes entries – their only failure during the season – and the sensational crash of Ascari's Lancia into Monte Carlo harbour when leading the race, because a brake locked. Ascari was recovered from the harbour apparently unhurt, the race was won by the Ferrari Tipo 625 of Maurice Trintignant and second place was taken by the Lancia of Eugenio

119 Stirling Moss' W196 which won the 1955 British Grand Prix at Aintree. Examples of the W196 can still be seen in various museums, including the Montagu Motor Museum.

120 Eugenio Castellotti drove this Lancia as a private entry in the 1955 Belgian Grand Prix, but retired with gearbox trouble. One of these cars is on display in the Turin Motor Museum.

121 The Tipo 555 Ferraris were further modified by Alberto Massimino for the 1955 Italian Grand Prix. Hawthorn is seen on the banking at Monza.

Castellotti. A week later Ascari was killed at the wheel of a sports Ferrari at Monza, when the car left the road and crashed for no apparent reason. Lancia was already in financial difficulties as the result of an over-ambitious competitions programme and Ascari's death was the final blow. The Turin Company immediately withdrew from racing, but Castellotti, ostensibly as a private owner, was allowed to drive one in the Belgian Grand Prix, where he retired with gearbox trouble. The cars, together with all equipment, spares and drawings were handed over to Enzo Ferrari, and provided a much-needed replacement for his unsuccessful 4-cylinder designs. The Lancias were henceforth entered as Ferraris and were raced throughout 1956 and 1957, during which time they were extensively modified. As Mercedes-Benz withdrew from racing at the end of 1955, the following season saw a resumption of the battle between Ferrari and Maserati, with the balance of success going in Ferrari's favour. Out of seven Grandes Epreuves held during the year, five were won by Ferrari and two by Maserati, while the two teams each gained the same number of second places.

There were, however, a number of interesting interlopers on the Grand Scene during 1956, and three of these were British. The first to appear was the Vanwall built by Tony Vandervell, the owner of the Ferrari 'Thin Wall Special' referred to earlier and very much of an advocate for the approach to Grand Prix design adopted by Ferrari. The car appeared originally as the 2-litre 'Vanwall Special' [figure 122] and had been intended for Formula Two, but was not ready in time. The Vanwall's 1,998 cc (86 × 86 mm) engine was a 4-cylinder design based on four Norton racing motor-cycle single cylinders with similar valve gear, and a crankcase and cylinder block built by Rolls-Royce for military purposes. In this form the car made its debut at the 1954 Daily Express Trophy meeting, but by the British Grand Prix it had a 2,237 cc engine and by the end of the season engine size had been increased to a full 2,490 cc (96 × 86 mm). The chassis closely followed Ferrari practice with a tubular frame built by Coopers, wishbones at the front, a de Dion axle at the rear, and using in both cases a transverse leaf spring. It was a car of simple, almost traditional, concept, but with two distinct advantages – Bosch fuel injection (from 1955), otherwise available only to Mercedes-Benz, and Goodyear single-pad disc brakes, developed from aircraft brakes, exclusive to Vanwall and vastly superior to the rival Dunlops. Two cars, known simply as 'Vanwalls' and fitted with double wishbone and coil spring front suspension, were raced during 1955 [figure 124]. They showed a considerable turn of speed, but were plagued by minor mechanical faults. For 1956 the cars were drastically revised and had a new multi-tubular space-frame designed by Colin Chapman of Lotus and a new and very aerodynamic body by Frank Costin. The rear suspension was redesigned and a 5-speed gearbox was fitted. During 1956 the make's only real success was a win in the *Daily Express* Trophy, but in the French Grand Prix at Rheims Harry Schell demonstrated that the Vanwall had the speed to match the Lancia-Ferraris, by passing two of them to hold second place for a short while. The Vanwall was destined to prove itself capable of great things in the future.

Built by the makers of the successful Formula Two car, the Formula One Connaught [figure 123], the prototype of which appeared in mid-1954, was a completely new design. The multi-tubular chassis had front suspension by wishbones and coil springs, while at the rear there was a de Dion axle and radius arms. Dunlop disc brakes and magnesium alloy wheels were fitted. The power unit was an Alta 4-cylinder twin overhead camshaft design, developed from the 2-litre engine, but much improved, with a capacity of 2,470 cc (93.5 × 90 mm) and a power output of 240 bhp at 7,000 rpm. In prototype form, SU fuel injection was used, but the complications of this were eventually abandoned in favour of Weber carburetters. Transmission was by a 4-speed Wilson pre-selector gearbox which was heavy, but had the advantage of permitting almost instantaneous gearchanges. The most novel feature of the Connaught was the all-enveloping aluminium body, divided at the waist so that the upper half could be lifted off completely, with a large stabilising fin.

The Connaught made its race debut early in 1955, but suffered from teething troubles throughout the year. Although the streamlined bodywork was far more functional than that fitted

122 As originally raced, the 1,998 cc 'Vanwall Special' was distinguished by a very unusual external tubular radiator. Alan Brown is seen driving the car at the 1954 *Daily Express* Trophy meeting at Silverstone.

123 Kenneth McAlpine with a streamlined car at the 1955 *Daily Express* Trophy Meeting at Silverstone. This body was rather more functional than the Mercedes.

to the Mercedes, for the driver was seated as though in a fighter aircraft and had excellent visibility, it was constantly being damaged in minor accidents and was expensive to repair. All three streamlined cars were rebuilt with conventional bodywork, and the first of these rebuilt works cars ran in the 1955 Syracuse Grand Prix held in October. Much to everyone's astonishment – especially that of the works Maserati team, the main opposition – the Connaught driven by Tony Brooks, a young dental student of very limited experience, scored Britain's first Grand Prix victory since Segrave's win with a Sunbeam at San Sebastian in 1924. Connaught was always desperately short of money and could afford to run in only a limited number of Continental events. Cars took third and fifth places in the 1956 Italian Grand Prix, but early in 1957 the team withdrew from racing and the cars were subsequently auctioned. Happily all the Syracuse models, as they became known after the 1955 victory, have survived and examples are from time to time seen in Historic Racing Car events.

The third new British car was the BRM [figure 126] which appeared at the end of 1955. After six years of battling with the complexities of the V-16 car, Mays and Berthon decided on a car that was simple in concept and of small overall dimensions. Like other British cars, the BRM had a 4-cylinder twin overhead camshaft engine of 2,497 cc (102·87 × 74·93 mm) and developing 248 bhp at 9,000 rpm. There was a multi-tubular space frame, front suspension by double wishbones with oleo-pneumatic struts, a de Dion rear axle and disc brakes of the conventional type at the front, but at the rear a single turbo-cooled transmission disc brake was mounted on the gearbox output shaft. Despite having many and good drivers, extensive development work and many mechanical changes, including the substitution of coil springs for the air struts, throughout the five years the cars were raced the only major successes gained were a win in the 1959 Dutch Grand Prix and second places in the 1958 Dutch and 1959 British events.

There also appeared at the end of the 1955 season a new car built by Gordini with an 8-cylinder in-line engine which he used in sports cars as well [figure 127]. This was a twin overhead

camshaft unit of conventional layout and had the low power output of 230 bhp which was quite insufficient to make it competitive. The simple tubular chassis had an identical system of independent suspension front and rear – of pivoting tubular arms and torsion bars. A 5-speed gearbox with synchromesh on the upper ratios was fitted and Messier disc brakes, mounted inboard at the rear, were used. Despite the new Gordini's undeniably good handling characteristics and enthusiastic driving by Hermanos de Silva Ramos and André Pilette, the make failed to achieve any worthwhile successes during 1956. In 1957 Amédée Gordini decided to give up the unequal struggle of racing without sufficient finance and took a job with Renault as a development engineer.

At this time were seen two other continental Grand Prix cars, each of which appeared in only one race. The first of these was the Arzani-Volpini which was a rebuild of one of the

124 (*above*) For 1955 Vandervell raced two cars and Harry Schell is seen in the British Grand Prix where the Vanwalls showed that they had the speed to match their Italian rivals, but were still plagued by minor mechanical troubles.

125 (*left*) The engine of the winning car at Syracuse in 1955. Note the 8-plug cylinder head, the twin-choke Weber carburetters with gauze covers over the intake trumpets and the wishbone front suspension.

126 (*left*) Like the Lancia, the BRM was short and squat and had an exceptionally good power output, but it proved notoriously unreliable. Here Harry Schell is seen in the 1959 British Grand Prix.

127 (*right*) For Gordini to produce a new car was something of a miracle. His 8-cylinder design handled well, but had not been fully developed by the time Gordini withdrew from racing in 1957. André Pilette in the 1956 *Daily Express* Trophy meeting at Silverstone.

Maserati-Milans referred to in chapter five. It had been fitted with a completely new body, a new 4-cylinder block of 2,496 cc (94 × 90 mm) and Weber carburetters. This was a rather amateur attempt at going Grand Prix racing and in the 1955 Pau Grand Prix, where it was driven by Mario Alborghetti, it crashed with fatal results for the driver.

In post-war days the Bugatti Company of Molsheim had produced only a very small number of cars and had made no serious attempt to restart production. It was with astonishment, therefore, that the racing car world viewed the new Bugatti Type 251 Grand Prix car [figures 128 and 129] that ran in the 1956 French Grand Prix. The design was the work of Giaocchino Colombo and again featured an in-line 8-cylinder engine, of 2,430 cc (75 × 68·8 mm). This engine was mounted transversely at the rear of the chassis, which meant that the car was very wide, but at the same time the wheelbase was very short. Power output was claimed to be 275 bhp at 9,000 rpm. The two cars built had many unusual features, not the least of which was non-independent suspension front and rear by de Dion axles. In the French race the car was driven by Maurice Trintignant, but it ran very slowly and the 251 made no further appearances.

Throughout 1957 Grand Prix racing was hotly contested between the Maserati, Lancia-Ferrari and Vanwall works cars. The v-8 Lancia-based cars had now been outpaced in development by their rivals and did not win a single Grande Epreuve during the year, although they scored a number of second places

and minor wins. The Maserati team was led by Juan Fangio and
the 250Fs had now been improved and developed in minor
ways, although the basic design remained unchanged, with the
result that they were both very fast and very reliable. Fangio
won the Argentine, Monaco, French and German Grands Prix
and gained his fifth win in the Drivers' Championship. The
Maserati concern had, however, realised in 1956 that their 250F
6-cylinder car was reaching the peak of its development life and
work was put in hand on a new design. They did not go to the
expense of designing a new chassis, but evolved a most elaborate sixty degree v-12 2,449 cc (68·7 × 56 mm) unit with twin
overhead camshafts per bank of cylinders, six twin-choke
carburetters and twenty-four sparking plugs and coils, which
would fit into the existing chassis. On the test bench 310 bhp
was developed at something over 10,000 rpm. The v-12 was
steadily developed throughout 1957, but was raced, without
success, at only Rheims and Monza. Maserati finally withdrew
from racing at the end of 1957, although they produced a light-
weight version of the 250F for 1958. The v-12 engine, however, formed the basis of that used in later sports/racing cars
and the unit which powered the 1966-7 Cooper-Maserati
Formula One cars.

For 1957 the Vanwalls had been developed to give a power
output of 290 bhp and coil spring rear suspension was fitted.
In the early part of the season, the cars showed that they were
the fastest Grand Prix cars racing, but they were still suffering
from minor mechanical failures. At the British Grand Prix, however, a Vanwall shared by Stirling Moss and Tony Brooks scored
Britain's first major Grand Prix victory since Segrave's win with
a Sunbeam at Tours in 1923 [figure 102], and this success was
followed by wins at Pescara and Monza. From the end of 1957
Grand Prix cars were obliged to run on 130-octane aviation fuel
instead of the former alcohol blends of their own choice, and
constructors had to considerably modify their engines. The
conversion of the Vanwall engine to 'Avgas' was particularly
difficult, as it relied to a greater extent than most cars on alcohol
for internal cooling. In its revised form 262 bhp was developed
at 7,500 rpm. During 1958, Vanwalls won four Grandes

128 This was the second of the two Type 251
Bugattis and was never raced.

129 The transversely mounted in-line
8-cylinder engine of the Type 251 Bugatti.
Note the 16-plug head, the four Weber
carburetters and the two four-branch exhaust
manifolds.

130 (*left*) One of the more valuable assets gained by Ferrari when he was given the Lancias was Vittorio Jano who designed for him the Dino V-6 Grand Prix car raced from 1958-60. Here Hawthorn is seen in the 1958 Portugese Grand Prix in which he finished second after a spin on the last lap.

131 (*right*) Too late and too heavy is a fair summing up of the Aston Martin DBR4. Carroll Shelby's car is seen here in the 1959 Italian Grand Prix.

Epreuves and gained the newly inaugurated Manufacturers' Championship. Vanwall withdrew from serious racing at the end of that year, but, later, cars were raced half-heartedly.

From 1958 until the end of the 2½-litre Formula, Ferrari raced a new v-6 model named the 'Dino' after his son and designed by Vittorio Jano [figure 130]. This had first appeared in 1957 in 1,489 cc Formula Two form, but by the end of that year engine capacity had been increased to 2,417 cc (85 × 71 mm) and power output was 290 bhp at 8,000 rpm. These cars, however, won only two Grandes Epreuves in 1958 and two in 1959, for they were facing severe opposition from new makes. Two of these, the Aston Martin and the American Scarab, could be discounted, as they were both heavy and out-dated when first raced. The Aston Martin DBR4/250 had a 2,492 cc (83 × 76·8 mm) engine developing approximately 280 bhp and in most respects closely followed the design of the Company's sports cars. The cars were first raced in 1959, but achieved very little success and the team withdrew from Grand Prix racing during the following season. The cars were sold in Australia with 3-litre engines, but two have now been re-imported and have been raced in British events by Peter Brewer. The other unsuccessful project was the Scarab, financed by the young American, Lance Reventlow. The Scarab's 4-cylinder 2,441 cc (85·25 × 85·73 mm) engine featured desmodromic valves and Hilborn-Travers fuel injection, and was mounted on its side at the front of the car to keep the overall height as low as possible. Alas, the cars were too heavy, too little developed and their drivers too inexperienced for the team to be competitive, and Reventlow returned to the United States after appearing at a few 1960 European events without success.

To the small Cooper concern must go the credit of taking over the role of keeping Britain to the forefront in Grand Prix racing after Vanwall had withdrawn. Since the first Cooper 500 cc racing car of 1946, the Company had concentrated on rear-engined cars, and when a new 1,500 cc Formula Two was introduced for 1957 Coopers built a rear-engined car with a Coventry-Climax single overhead camshaft engine to comply with it. Coventry-Climax introduced a twin-cam engine and this was progressively increased in capacity to a full 2,495 cc [figure 132]. After unexpected wins by Stirling Moss with a 1·9-litre Cooper in the 1958 Argentine Grand Prix and by Maurice Trintignant at Monaco that year, a works-entered

132 Although not recognised as an Historic Racing Car, the rear-engined Cooper-Climax made such an impact on the racing scene that it must be regarded as one of the most historic and important designs of all time. Jack Brabham, World Champion at the wheel of a Cooper in 1959 and 1960, is seen in the 1960 Oulton Park Gold Cup.

133 Light, fast and with superb handling, the Mk. XVI Lotus represented Colin Chapman's very scientific approach to Grand Prix racing. As many as four of these cars at a time have appeared in Historic Racing Car events.

Cooper driven by Jack Brabham won two Grandes Epreuves and gained sufficient places for him to win the 1959 Drivers' World Championship. This he repeated in 1960 with six wins in Grandes Epreuves. By Grand Prix standards the Cooper was a simple design, but it was also highly effective and radical. By 1960 the rear-engined layout had been imitated by BRM, Ferrari and Lotus. The Vintage Sports Car Club, however, who organise the majority of Historic Racing Car events in Britain, do not accept rear-engined cars in their events.

The Climax engine in its various forms was also used by the British Lotus Company, who built a front-engined Formula Two car for the 1957 season. This featured a multi-tubular 'space-frame' chassis with suspension by double wishbones at the front and by the famous 'strut' suspension designed by the Company's chief, Colin Chapman, at the rear. With the strut system there was a drive shaft which located the wheel later-ally, a radius arm facing forwards, a coil spring and a damper strut member, all converging into an aluminium casing behind the wheel. Transmission was by a 5-speed constant mesh gear-box and incorporated a ZF limited slip differential. During 1957 the cars were regularly raced in Formula Two events, and when a 2-litre Climax engine became available for 1958 Chapman ran the cars in the majority of the year's Formula One races. From this model was developed the much improved Mk 16 [figure 133] which had a body styled by Frank Costin, who had been responsible for the Vanwall body, and was raced in some events with a canted engine. The great potential of the cars was ruined by a succession of transmission, overheating and carburation troubles. The 16 first appeared at the 1958 French Grand Prix and in two seasons its best performance was fourth place in the 1959 Dutch Grand Prix; in 1960, the model was superseded by the rear-engined Mk 18. Several of the front-engined cars have survived, however, and they are frequently seen in Historic Racing Car events.

The 2½-litre Formula was popular with both entrants and spectators and during its seven years many technical advances took place. A large number of the cars have survived and are often seen racing. They still provide an exciting spectacle of sound and speed.